Unnatural Disaster

Also edited by
BETSY REED

*Nothing Sacred: Women Respond to Religious
Fundamentalism and Terror*

Unnatural Disaster

The Nation
ON HURRICANE
KATRINA

Edited by
BETSY REED

Introduction by
ADOLPH REED, JR.

NATION
BOOKS

Nation Books
New York

Published by
Nation Books
An Imprint of Avalon Publishing Group, Inc.
245 West 17th Street, 11th Floor
New York, NY 10011

NATION
BOOKS

Copyright © 2006 *The Nation*

Introduction © 2006 Adolph Reed, Jr.

Nation Books is a co-publishing venture of The Nation Institute and Avalon Publishing Group Incorporated.

Library of Congress Cataloging-in-Publication Data

ISBN-10: 1-56025-937-X

ISBN-13: 978-1-56025-937-4

9 8 7 6 5 4 3 2 1

Book design by Pauline Neuwirth, Neuwirth & Associates, Inc.

Printed in the United States of America

Distributed by Publishers Group West

Contents

EDITOR'S NOTE   ix

INTRODUCTION: *Adolph Reed, Jr.*   xiii

Part One: STURM UND DRANG   1

THE VIEW FROM LOTT'S PORCH *by Patricia J. Williams*   3

THE BIG EASY DIES HARD *by Christian Parenti*   7

FEMA: CONFEDERACY OF DUNCES *by Jon Elliston*   13

GLOBAL STORM WARNING *by Mark Hertsgaard*   17

LOOTING THE BLACK POOR *by Earl Ofari Hutchinson*   23

CLASS-IFYING THE HURRICANE *by Adolph Reed, Jr.*   27

BREAD, ROSES, AND THE FLOOD *by Eric Foner*   33

BOHEMIA'S LAST FRONTIER *by Curtis Wilkie*   35

LEVEE TOWN *by Alexander Cockburn*   41

THE REAL COSTS OF A
    CULTURE OF GREED *by Robert Scheer*   45

FOUND IN THE FLOOD *by Eric Alterman*   49

THE DISASTER PRESIDENT *by The Editors*   53

Part Two: THE LOOTING OF NEW ORLEANS   57

PURGING THE POOR *by Naomi Klein*   59

    DOING THE MATH *by Naomi Klein and Aaron Maté*   67

    GOP OPPORTUNITY ZONE   69

BLACKWATER DOWN *by Jeremy Scahill*   73

PAT ROBERTSON'S KATRINA CASH *by Max Blumenthal*   81

KATRINA AND THE COMING
    WORLD OIL CRUNCH *by Michael T. Klare*   89

THE RECONSTRUCTION OF NEW ORAQ
    by Tom Engelhardt and Nick Turse   95

LEFT TO DIE *by Billy Sothern*   109

Part Three: A PEOPLE'S RECONSTRUCTION   117

HURRICANE GUMBO *by Mike Davis and Anthony Fontenot*   119

BEYOND SHELTERS *by Michael Tisserand*   133

A SECOND-LINE REVIVAL *by Billy Sothern*   139

LET THE PEOPLE REBUILD
    NEW ORLEANS *by Naomi Klein*   147

NEW ORLEANS: RAZE OR REBUILD? *by Christian Parenti*   153

A "New" New Deal *by William Greider* — 161

History Lessons
by Katrina vanden Heuvel — 165

Visionaries Wanted *by Nicholas von Hoffman* — 171

Prez on the Precipice *by The Editors* — 173

Part Four: After the Flood — 177

25 Questions about the Murder
of New Orleans *by Mike Davis and Anthony Fontenot* — 179

In the Shadow of Disaster *by Ari Kelman* — 187

Katrina Lives *by Susan Straight* — 195

New Orleans Blues *by The Editors* — 203

Hard Times in the Big Easy *by Gary Younge* — 207

Bush's New Storm *by Michael Tisserand* — 211

Neglect in New Orleans *by The Editors* — 215

Suppressing the N.O. Vote *by The Editors* — 219

The Battle of New Orleans *by Gary Younge* — 223

Contributors — 227

Index — 233

Acknowledgments — 241

Editor's Note

A YEAR AFTER Hurricane Katrina, New Orleans lies in ruins. While the cable TV shows roll out their commemorative logos, nearly 400,000 of the city's residents remain displaced and dispersed, and only a tiny proportion of the promised $30 billion in federal aid has been delivered. Just as, in the weeks following the storm, the crumbled levees, bloated bodies, and flooded neighborhoods were painful symbols of government neglect, today's wreckage speaks eloquently of official lies and broken promises.

Katrina was a natural disaster that, like a pitiless X-ray, laid bare the unnatural disaster of our political system. For a moment, it appeared that the hurricane might provide an occasion to change the very patterns it exposed, having ripped off the facade that for so many years allowed the nation's political class to betray its citizens without consequence—abandoning poor urban communities; consigning their children to decrepit schools; weakening public institutions in a perverse (yet effective) quest to demonize government and boost the political fortunes of those who regard it with contempt. With Katrina, the incompetence of the federal response was so staggering, the inhumanity so extreme that all of a sudden, policies and priorities that hadn't seemed especially important to many Americans were unacceptable. The pathetic FEMA, and its bumbling head, Michael Brown, became a late-night laugh line. Bush and his cronies—given a free pass by the same media when they launched their rampage in Iraq—were finally on the run.

Of course, the shamefaced politicos pointing fingers and making vows were chiefly concerned with saving their own skins, as became clear in the halting and corruption-ridden "reconstruction" process and in the sham "investigation" into federal missteps conducted by the GOP-controlled Congress. And the conspicuous failures of the governing party only made the weakness and complicity of the supposed opposition party more glaring. Also, as Adolph Reed, Jr. argues in the introduction to this volume, commentators of all stripes were more likely to lament the racial disparities on display in the storm's aftermath than they were to grapple with the poisonous legacy of the neoliberal economic project, which rendered New Orleans's poor, largely black population so vulnerable in the first place.

Nonetheless, the social catastrophe both revealed and exacerbated by the hurricane placed those most directly responsible in the hot seat, creating a moment ripe for political journalism. This is a collection of articles that appeared in *The Nation* and on its website in response to that moment. It includes reported pieces that surveyed the damage in the Gulf; commentary sifting through the outrages and absurdities and flashes of courage in Washington; and essays by longtime New Orleanians—including author Curtis Wilkie, former *Gambit Weekly* editor Michael Tisserand, and anti-death-penalty lawyer Billy Sothern—on the city's past, present, and future. The contributors do not share a uniform political or analytical point of view; as they wrestle with questions like the significance of race, relative to class, in determining who bore the brunt of the suffering—and how and whether all of New Orleans should be rebuilt—they sometimes come to different conclusions. What they have in common is a determination to cut through the official lies and deceit, the glib rhetoric and the pieties, to get to the bottom of what happened in New Orleans—not only to hold to account the hacks and the cronies and the public officials all the way to the top, but to find out how the stage was set for them to do such damage.

Thus, along with pieces on "The Disaster President" and "Pat Robertson's Katrina Cash" and the Bush administration's gutting of FEMA, there are essays here about the condition of the black poor in New Orleans before Katrina, the long-term degradation of Louisana's wetlands, and the brutality of prisons in the Big Easy, where sheriff's deputies left terrified inmates to drown in their jail cells as the floodwaters rose. There are exposés of the outrageous cronyism that flourished in the post-storm period, when Republican-connected companies like Blackwater USA and Halliburton, notorious for their warmaking and profiteering in Iraq, reaped the bounty of federal contracts in New Orleans. But there are also stories about places like Evangeline Parish, Louisiana, where Mike Davis and Anthony Fontenot found a community completely bereft of government and charitable assistance cobbling together a heroic homemade relief and rescue operation. And there are impassioned editorials, by William Greider and Katrina vanden Heuvel, calling for a "New" New Deal for the region—a modernized version of FDR's WPA to rebuild the public infrastructure and renew the social contract whose breach was made so terribly vivid by the hurricane.

While the magazine's journalists reported on the corruption and ineptitude of the rebuilding process, they kept their eyes on the prize: the entitlement of the hurricane's victims to just treatment and a voice in their own future—including control over the funds collected in their names. As columnist Naomi Klein argued, the money raised by private charities and released by Congress rightfully belonged not to the relief agencies or the government but to the victims—as she put it, referring to the infamous quip by the President's mother about evacuees at Houston's Astrodome, "the people Barbara Bush tactfully described as 'underprivileged anyway' just got very rich." Subsequent articles reported on the contest that ensued over control of the rebuilding process and its resources, pitting grassroots evacuees' groups against the emerging post-storm power structure in New Orleans.

It is certainly worthwhile to recall the humiliation of Bush, Brown, Chertoff, and Co. in the immediate wake of the hurricane, as many of these articles do. But it is in the struggles for justice by its victims that the legacy of Katrina will ultimately be decided.

BETSY REED

Introduction

As of late May 2006, nine months after Hurricane Katrina came ashore, bodies are still being found amid the storm's detritus in New Orleans. The running Louisiana death toll has surpassed 1,500, mostly in Orleans Parish. According to a Brookings Institution report, *Katrina Index: Tracking Variables of Post-Katrina Recovery*, by February the city's population had rebounded to more than 181,000—up from 139,000 last November, down from between 463,000 and 480,000 on August 29.

Dollar figures in the incomprehensible billions have been assigned to the total damage. We have been told repeatedly and in definitive tones by gushing talking heads where New Orleans and Katrina in general rank on the all-time list of American catastrophes—none of which, of course, conveys any real sense of what has occurred or its impact on the city and its people.

I have a vivid sense of that impact. The city that I've known all my life will never be the same. Nearly all my family there was or remains displaced. My mother checked in to a downtown hotel with other relatives on August 28. She didn't see her house again until October 19; her neighborhood sat in four feet of water for nearly a month after the 17th Street Canal ruptured. She couldn't move back home until New Year's Day. Some family members were more fortunate, some less. Most of them lived in the Gentilly area, which was largely inundated by the breach of the London Avenue Canal. Even some whose houses weren't flooded remain displaced, as children had no schools, and most of the city was without electricity and other services.

However, as terrible as this has been for all of us, my extended family's experience underscores the significance of the safety net that class—as income, wealth, and access to material resources, including a supportive fabric of social connections— provides. Most evacuated the city before the storm. None of those who chose to ride it out in the city wound up marooned and abandoned in the Superdome or convention center. And unlike many who remained, they really did choose to stay; they had plausible options. My mother is retired with a good pension to augment her Social Security benefits and a house that she owns without mortgage debt. All the adults are homeowners and professionals of one sort or another whose jobs and livelihoods weren't swept away with the storm. All had resources to define the terms of their displacement and live as refugees in relatively comfortable and secure circumstances. And their situation is by no means extraordinary among the city's black population.

In the wake of the storm, the images projected in the mass media of the people who were warehoused in the Superdome and the convention center, stranded on rooftops, and stuck without food and water on the parched overpasses seemed to cry out a stark statement of racial inequality. But as I argue in my contribution to this volume, class was certainly a better predictor than race of who evacuated the city before the hurricane, who was able to survive the storm itself, who remained in shelters in Houston or elsewhere, whose interests will be factored into the reconstruction of the city, who will be able to return. This is not to say that race does not play a significant role in shaping the social and economic hierarchy in New Orleans; racial hierarchy has been a conspicuous, constitutive element of the city's history and politics practically from its founding. It is to say that racism is not an adequate conceptual frame for understanding Katrina's impact or the bases of the struggles that will determine the city's future. It is not even an adequate frame for understanding the sources and dynamics reproducing the inequalities that appear most conspicuously along racial lines.

There is clearly no lack of racial inequality, or frankly racist ideology for that matter, in New Orleans. But the inequality and injustice seemed to be so dramatically reducible to race partly because in the contemporary United States race is the most familiar language of inequality and injustice. It's what we see partly because it's what we're accustomed to seeing, what we look for even without being conscious of doing so. The racial critique, though, cannot help expose or make sense of the deeper structures of neoliberal practice and ideology that underlie everything about the travesty in New Orleans, as well as the other devastated areas of the Gulf Coast. (St. Bernard Parish, adjacent to the Lower Ninth Ward, 90 percent white, working-class, and reliably Republican, was virtually wiped off the face of the earth. Most of the parish's housing was destroyed. No hospitals, public libraries, or childcare facilities have opened yet, and only 7 percent of its schools are operating.)

Many liberals gravitate to the language of racism both because it makes them feel righteous and because it doesn't carry any political warrant beyond exhorting people not to be racist or lamenting that they are. In fact, it often is exactly the opposite of a call to action. Such formulations as "racism is our national disease" or similar pieties imply that racism is a natural condition, that most whites inevitably and immutably oppose blacks and therefore can't be expected to align with them around common political goals. This view helps to make sense of Democrats' persistent commitment—despite repeated failure—to an electoral strategy centered on appeals to an upper-income white constituency concerned primarily with issues like abortion rights and the deficit. Focus on that constituency, given a different name for each election, partly reflects the usually tacit suspicion that a social justice agenda is hopelessly stigmatized by association with blacks. (Of course, the fact that corporations and Wall Street aren't so crazy about social justice is no doubt also a factor.) Upper-status liberals are more likely to have relatively secure, rewarding jobs, access to healthcare, adequate housing, and prospects for providing for the kids' education, and are much less likely to be in danger of being sent to Iraq. They tend, therefore, to have a higher threshold of tolerance for political compromises on those issues in the name of electing this year's Democrat. Acknowledging racism—along with being pro-choice, of course—is one of the few ways many of them can distinguish themselves from their Republican co-workers and relatives.

Insistence on understanding inequality fundamentally in racial terms is a vestige of an earlier political style. The discourse of race politics persists among progressives partly out of habit, partly because it connects with the material interests of those who would be race relations technicians. Almost everyone agrees that racism is bad; that's a reflection of the last half-century's victories in the struggle for social justice. There is no consensus, however, on what counts as racism, how to define its boundaries, or how to overcome it. Yet the fact that this discourse is so ambiguous may well be an element of its appeal; debating whether some act, incident, or social relation should be considered racist conveniently directs attention away from other, no less consequential metrics of justice. In one simple example, many black landlords in New Orleans were as eager as their white counterparts to evict displaced tenants. How does the standard of racial justice inform a struggle over the limits of property rights in cases where both owner and tenant are black? Tellingly, those who insist on interpreting the differential impact of the storm and its aftermath in the language of racism—like Manning Marable in "New Orleans Reconsidered: Race or Class?"—merely catalogue racially disparate outcomes, offering no larger analysis.

Simply noting the existence of racial disparities, or even cataloguing them systematically, does not persuasively demonstrate injustice or mobilize remedial action. The presumption that it does reflects progressives' insularity. The jury verdict in the first Rodney King trial should have long since driven home the point that only those who already are inclined to believe that racism is the source of inequality accept that charge. Jurors watched a group of cops relentlessly beat and shock a prostrate King and determined that he was attacking them. Everyone sees what they expect to see, and the right has ready counters to assertions that the dramatic racial disparities Katrina exposed in New Orleans are evidence of racial injustice. Rightist ideologues immediately mobilized all the scurrilous racial stereotypes that they have propagated all along to justify attacks on civil rights, social protection, and government responsibility. They proffered alternative explanations that attributed existing disparities to black deficiencies rather than injustice. Ironically, making race the unit of analysis helps the right make racial difference the issue.

Reducing political critique to the language of racial disparity reinforces inequality by obscuring its sources. Liberals' policy discourse exacerbates this problem and tacitly legitimizes right-wing arguments by linking poverty and culture. Again New Orleans is instructive. More than 200 prominent liberal social scientists—including William Julius Wilson and former Clinton administration welfare reformers David Ellwood and Mary Jo Bane—signed a statement calling for the federal government to take advantage of the opportunity to "deconcentrate" poverty from New Orleans and the Gulf Coast. Their pro forma demurral about not wanting to "depopulate the city of its historically black communities" amounts to a sleight of hand; it is entirely possible to preserve "historically black communities" while sweeping large numbers of poor people out of them. As Stephen Steinberg and I pointed out in *The Black Commentator*, in post-Katrina New Orleans as elsewhere the rhetoric of deconcentrating poverty rationalizes real estate developers' schemes for displacing poor people to make way for upscale housing and commercial projects. Stunningly, the social scientists circulated their statement without taking account of the fact that Joe Canizaro—billionaire real estate developer, Bush Pioneer ($100,000+ campaign supporter), and key member of

Mayor Ray Nagin's Bring New Orleans Back Commission (BNOB)—and other developers were already jockeying to define the future of the city as a luxury theme park. Nor did they consider the ways that their relocation scheme could rationalize wholesale involuntary displacement.

Fixation on "deconcentrating" poverty stems from the notion that black poor people largely are mired in a culturally defective urban underclass; it also presumes that such people have no legitimate commitment to place. As it always has, this sort of cultural stigmatization perfumes a brutal system in which effective rights are a direct function of possession of marketable assets. Possession of assets may be to some extent a proxy for race; however, race is also a proxy for possession of assets. It is possible simultaneously to deal black people in and poor people out. Casting the debate over displaced New Orleanians' right of return in narrowly racial terms, rather than as a presumptive right of citizenship, leaves space to sidestep this crucial issue. And it has been sidestepped.

The initial recommendation for reconstructing the city was presented to Nagin's BNOB by the Urban Land Institute, a real estate industry association created in the 1930s to combat public housing, and of which Canizaro is a trustee. Commissioning the ULI to prepare a rebuilding plan is like hiring Jesse James as a bank guard. Its report called for a form of triage that would give priority to areas with high property values. It also recommended that rebuilding in the Lower Ninth Ward and New Orleans East, heavily black neighborhoods worst hit by the flooding, be postponed indefinitely, if not precluded outright. This recommendation, along with a short time frame that Nagin and the BNOB initially proposed for displaced residents to return to save their homes from demolition, generated an uproar and protest from displaced residents that was expressed partly in racial terms. Especially people from the East and the Lower Ninth Ward feared a de facto alliance between developers who want to clear as much land as possible and those whites who made no bones about wanting to reconstruct the city without a black majority. Residents of Little Vietnam in the East reacted to a plan to locate a landfill in their badly flood-damaged neighborhood, and others across the city objected that the time frame for reclaiming and redeeming property was too brief.

As he's done on several occasions since the storm, Nagin retreated in the face of the protest. The "Chocolate City" quip for which he became notorious nationally was an instance of his scuffling to reassure angry black New Orleanians that he did not endorse the models of a smaller, whiter city that were being touted widely and that seemed to follow from his administration's utterances and practices. And it is revealing of the depth and persistence of many whites' racial double standards that the mayor's affirmation of the goal of retaining a black majority provoked a national and local firestorm of denunciation as narrow and racist, but the many calls for remaking New Orleans as a white-majority city, to which he was ultimately responding, generated no such reaction.

However, Nagin's main concession to protest against the ULI proposal was to extend greater latitude to "homeowners." The simplistic racial critique of the rebuilding plan obscured the reality that, in what was supposed to be a victory for popular interests against developers, renters were left out of the equation entirely and thus established as non-stakeholders, with no recognized claims in a discussion of the city's future or their right to a place in it. The irony is that blacks were disproportionately renters, and renters were disproportionately black. And roughly 90 percent of rental units destroyed were low-income affordable housing. Many, no doubt a preponderance, of black homeowners are not affluent, and securing greater civic voice for homeowners democratized the process, if only by slowing down the development juggernaut a bit. Nevertheless, the concession at the same time inscribed property ownership as the condition for entry into the arena of interest groups with effective civic voice.

Treating property ownership as the sine qua non for policy consideration didn't raise any eyebrows locally or nationally—except among the ranks of those who were left out. Neither the black mayor nor the majority black city council has shown initiative in taking into account, much less defending, the interests of poor New Orleanians. The city's evacuation plans notoriously failed to anticipate adequately poor people's circumstances and needs. Landlords began evicting tenants without a hint of due process as soon as water receded and rumors spread of possibilities for extracting exorbitant rents from construction workers. The state officially prohibited evictions before October 25, but that prohibition was academic for the tens of thousands of people dispersed in shelters around the region and the nation. And even that minimal right was flagrantly ignored with impunity.

Council president Oliver Thomas complained in February that government programs and agencies have "pampered" poor people and proclaimed that they should not be encouraged to return. As he put it, "We don't need soap opera watchers right now." At least one other black council member expressed

support of his view, as did the New Orleans Housing Authority (HANO) receiver. To complete the circle, the HANO
receiver, who is also black, is a professional housing authority
hack with a background in the Moving to Opportunity programs that the social scientists proclaimed as the basis for a
wonderful opportunity to resettle the poor. This all attests to
the triumph of neoliberalism as both ideology and policy
regime, and that triumph is seamlessly compatible with the discourse of racial politics. Black property owners, after all, are
stakeholders as well as whites.

In *A Brief History of Neoliberalism*, David Harvey quotes
Margaret Thatcher's succinct statement of the neoliberal ideological program: "Economics are the method, but the object is
to change the soul." The goal of this change is acceptance, as
the unquestioned natural order of things, that private is always
better than public, and that the main functions of government are to enhance opportunities for the investor class and suppress wages for everyone else. Katrina and reactions to it throw
into relief how successful that program has been.

In October 2005, returning from my first trip to New
Orleans since the week before the storm, I wound up in conversation with a fortysomething white doctor who lives in Jackson, Mississippi. As a native Floridian, she had a sense of the
damage that a Category 4 or 5 storm could produce even as far
inland as Jackson; so, when Katrina was upgraded the weekend
before landfall, she headed for the city's main storm shelter to
volunteer. She was shocked when she arrived to find that no
other doctors had volunteered. She expressed surprise and dis-
may that "people just didn't step up." When I suggested that's
one reason we need a strong central government, to mobilize

responses to such crises, she immediately and animatedly dissented that she doesn't believe in "big government." When I asked who, then, was to have "stepped up," her response was vague—individual doctors, unspecified voluntary groups. She literally had no conception that there are some things that only large public institutions can do in a centrally organized way. When we changed the topic to maintain civility, I learned that she was going to visit her son, a student at the University of Pennsylvania. On hearing that's where I teach, she related with glee that the previous semester her progeny had taken a course on Tupac Shakur: "Only at Penn, right?" That's one facet of the neoliberal mindset; it can be broadening and culturally enriching to spend $40,000 a year for a child to learn about a dead rapper, but a counterproductive use of resources to fund government and public services. This brings to mind Thatcher's other, more infamous quip, that there's "no such thing as society, only individual men and women and their families."

This view, which the late Daniel Singer memorialized as TINA—There Is No Alternative to market logic – has become the default position of common sense. Its smug moral standard, really only a template for self-righteous opportunism, is drawn from an idealized world in which equivalent individuals make choices in line with an abstract market rationality. Its viciousness seeped through even during the phase of mass-mediated compassion for the human suffering in New Orleans. The litany of victim-blaming questions frequently enough arose: why didn't they evacuate? Why would they choose to live below sea level? Why should we be expected to pay for their choices? Those questions no doubt had a racial edge regarding New Orleans, but it is useful to recall that Joseph Allbaugh,

Michael Brown's predecessor as FEMA director, denigrated FEMA as a huge "entitlement program" when he took over and promptly stonewalled rural white, heavily Republican Missourians with the same kind of accusatory language during the severe floods of 2001.

As the arresting television images that sparked a Hallmark card moment of collective sympathy recede farther down the memory hole, what remains of Katrina discourse is largely the trope of victim-blaming interrogation. To qualify for our sympathy, victims of natural disasters now must reassure us that their bad choices aren't to blame. CNN coverage of a recent spate of destructive tornadoes in Texas began with the question, Why do these people live in tornado-prone country without basements? The ground is too hard, and the costs are prohibitive. Whew! I guess it's okay to empathize with them, and maybe they deserve some assistance after all.

However, as Harvey points out, despite its free-market utopianism, neoliberalism depends on the existence of the public sector as a source of raw material for commoditization. It is largely a program of privatization for which public resources are equivalent to nature's bounty in Enlightenment liberalism. Thus Allbaugh's complaint about entitlement was prelude to his outsourcing much of the agency's functions with sweetheart contracts to corporate cronies.

Demonizing government to cut public spending and regulation, plundering the public treasury through privatization, and rationalizing both through the myth of magical market efficiency all underlie what happened to New Orleans. The storm exposed the consequences of neoliberalism's lies and mystifications, in a single locale and all at once.

The levees on the 17th Street and London Avenue canals, it turns out, failed because they were inadequately constructed. In the words of the Independent Levee Investigation Team, "safety was exchanged for efficiency and reduced costs." This was largely the result of federal underfunding, partly the result of the Army Corps of Engineers's skimping, partly state and local officials' temporizing and lack of adequate government oversight (or, in neoliberal parlance, cutting government red tape). The breach of the Industrial Canal, as well as much of the flooding of St. Bernard Parish, resulted largely from storm surge that pushed up the Mississippi River Gulf Outlet, a boondoggle channel dug four decades ago as corporate welfare that was obsolete almost from its opening.

It's certainly understandable that Mayor Nagin found himself overwhelmed and that he occasionally lost composure in the first days of a sui generis disaster, and the negative comparisons to Giuliani's handling of 9/11 are absurd, if not racist twaddle. I took the subway with no problem to my office, not much more than a mile up Fifth Avenue from the World Trade Center, and then walked to my apartment in Alphabet City, on 9/12. Nearly all of New Orleans's infrastructure was destroyed, overwhelmed or inaccessible after the levees failed; not even most of Manhattan below 14th Street was in that condition after the World Trade Center collapse.

Nagin's finest moments were his no-nonsense denunciations of the Bush administration's dereliction and his passionate demands for federal assistance. Nevertheless, at every point the mayor has been hamstrung and undone by his commitment to a neoliberal approach to government. Less than two months before Katrina, the Nagin administration determined that it couldn't afford to provide transportation to evacuate. So the city produced DVDs to distribute in poor neighborhoods, alerting residents that they would be on their own in the event of a major storm. Since then, Nagin and other local officials have governed unwaveringly in line with neoliberal presumptions, even as doing so may have stifled repopulation and reconstruction. First, while the city was still submerged, Nagin fired 3,000 municipal employees, many, if not most, of whom had lost their homes or been displaced. Later, the Orleans Parish School Board laid off 7,500 teachers and other employees. No serious consideration was given to the possibility that maintaining a public workforce could help people return sooner by giving them income, providing services, and augmenting the cleanup and reconstruction efforts. Nine months after the storm, municipal services remained barely existent. Only 21 percent of schools in Orleans Parish were open. Most of those are operating as charter schools, as privatizers have seized the moment. Only 49 percent of bus routes and 17 percent of buses in New Orleans were in service. My family and countless others attest to the hassle of trying to deal with the irrationality of privatized utilities companies. Still, both mayor and council can imagine only scenarios in which the "private sector" will be stimulated to come to the rescue and lead a renaissance. This means that they can imagine only policies aimed at boosting investor confidence— cutting spending precisely when they should be increasing it—or drawing on corporate "expertise."

And this isn't just a New Orleans thing. St. Bernard Parish, practically without revenue, has outsourced much of its police service, bringing in Dyncorp, a private military services firm— what used to be called mercenaries. It's difficult to understand how paying them at least three to four times more (some estimates run as high as $950 per man per day) than the local deputies with whom they'll be grouped will save money. Governor Blanco in the days after the storm hired Blackwater USA, another such firm, to provide "security" in New Orleans, during the period when subsequently disproven rumors of chaos and widespread violence titillated the nation and fueled the right's pornographic racism. The state even outsourced identification of bodies after the hurricane, in some cases, apparently, to firms with histories of fraud and misfeasance.

It's at the federal level, where the responsibility should be heaviest in times of such great disaster, as well as for preventing it in the first place, that the practical realization of neoliberal vision is most striking. The Bush administration's refusal, in the face of overwhelming evidence of the danger, to fund the New Orleans levee project is well known and criminal. Michael Brown's incompetence and lack of engagement became breathtakingly clear to the public shortly after Katrina's landfall. His e-mail records from the time show just how cynical his appointment was. They also bring to mind Hannah Arendt's description of the banality of evil. As Katrina steamed through the Gulf, Brown hesitated to declare a disaster area in its Florida wake, expressing concern that some might file fraudulent claims. Presumably for the same reason he temporized until the storm had come ashore on the Gulf Coast. On August 29, hours after the storm hit Louisiana, he issued a press statement urging us all to contribute to a list of sixteen recommended private charities to support relief efforts. That was a strange enough abdication of his responsibility as director of the federal agency charged with managing emergencies, but the

Red Cross was the only secular agency on the list. On
August 31, responding to a memo alerting him to critical conditions at the Superdome and Convention Center, he wrote,
"Thanks for the update. Anything specific I need to do or
tweak?" A few hours later he replied to a frustrated staffer in
the field, "I'm working on an organization chart and staffing
plan now." During those days he found time to respond to e-
mails from random citizens either praising or criticizing his
efforts and forward them, along with self-pitying comments, to
his staff.

Brown was in over his head. But the larger point is that he
and his bosses—Chertoff and Bush—have so little regard for
government that they couldn't conceive of the agency's functions, even to go through the motions. They could connect only
to do public relations damage control, punish enemies, and out-
source plunder to cronies. When the chief executive officers of
the eight parishes hardest hit by Katrina and then Rita participated in a discussion on local public television in late October
2005, each of them—and all except Nagin and Jefferson Parish
executive Aaron Broussard are Republicans—was trenchantly
critical of FEMA's shoddy performance (and the Red Cross's, by
the way). They also complained bitterly about Halliburton
and the other private contractors the Bush administration had
hired to do cleanup. The main charge was that the firms refused
to coordinate with others and had demanded additional pay for
every action. Such is the practical truth of "market efficiency."

As time goes on, fewer and fewer Americans will recall that
government can do anything but make war and suppress dissent. And neither the labor movement (in either flavor);
women's civil rights, and environmentalist groups; nor least of

all the Democratic Party seems prepared to advance and fight for a clear alternative vision. In this context, the struggle for New Orleans's future may be a more extreme, condensed version of the future of many, many more people as the bipartisan neoliberal consensus reduces government to a tool of corporations and the investor class alone.

New Orleans is a predominantly black city, and it is a largely poor city; the black population is disproportionately poor, and the poor population is disproportionately black. It is not surprising and certainly no simple coincidence that those who were stranded and forgotten, probably those who died, were conspicuously black. It's also the case that many, perhaps even most, whites would prefer that the city lose its black majority—or think they would until they yearn to condescend in watching small kids tap dance on the street corner, need to hear some music, or have someone bring a cool, tropical drink. And it is true that race has been a crucial metaphor through which politics and power have been enacted there.

But does condensing interpretation of the regime of inequality on which the city has been built into the discourse of racism help us understand that regime or struggle effectively against it? What does that discourse help explain, and what doesn't it explain? What strategic or programmatic possibilities follow from it? I believe the case of Katrina underscores that in the most important ways, for making sense of this world and fighting for a better one, it clouds more than it clarifies.

We must also be wary of arguments that New Orleans should be preserved because of its unique cultural heritage. The cultural uniqueness argument rests on a dangerous and self-defeating exceptionalism that subordinates all other notions of justice to the utilitarian market calculus. Should Chalmette, Bay St. Louis, and Pass Christian not be rebuilt because they don't have King Zulu, Mardi Gras Indians, and Mulé's hot sausage po' boys? In emphasizing the city's distinctness, this defense is also the flip side of an argument for not funding reconstruction: I didn't choose to live in that alien place below sea level; why should I pay for your irresponsibility?

New Orleans should be rebuilt and New Orleanians' right to return should be supported not because of any potted multiculturalism—itself a neoliberal spawn—two steps removed from exoticist fantasy and the convention and Tourism Bureau's sales effort. That rhetoric, furthermore, plays into the forces that would rebuild the city as a theme park. It should be rebuilt for the same reasons that disaster relief should go to other places hit by tornadoes, earthquakes, forest fires, and other floods: because protection and repair from catastrophe must be an entitlement for everyone in the society, as a condition of membership. It's time to take a clear stand for social solidarity.

ADOLPH REED, JR.
MAY 2006

ONE

Sturm und Drang

The View from Lott's Porch

by Patricia J. Williams

[from the September 26, 2005 issue]

WHEN I THINK about the human disaster in the wake of Hurricane Katrina, there are two moments that stand out in my mind. The first is George W. Bush's press conference in Mississippi on September 2, during which he bounced uneasily from foot to foot like he couldn't wait to get out of there, looking sullen and furrowed, observing with tense jocularity that Trent Lott's house had been lost, too, and that "we" were going to rebuild him "a fantastic house" and that he, our President, was looking forward to rocking on the porch when that day came to pass. The second moment was the now-famous interview with Homeland Security chief Michael Chertoff on National Public Radio. Media junkie that I am, I had the TV and the radio on at the same time. As pictures of the horrific conditions at the convention center, including the image of that poor old woman who had passed away in her wheelchair, were being broadcast to the world, Chertoff was insisting that he had no knowledge of any extreme conditions or deaths at the center. "Our reporter has seen [it]," insisted the host. "I can't argue with you about what your reporter tells you," said Chertoff.

I confess that I find myself filtering this horror through a very personal lens. It overlaps with the task of clearing out and selling the house I grew up in, the house my mother was born in, my grandmother's house, a house that has belonged to my family for a hundred years. My distress at having to give it up is confused with the scenes of Katrina's devastation that most of us—if not Chertoff—are witnessing. Against that appalling backdrop I find myself clinging to a sense of place, even though I am not truly or traumatically displaced. Mine was an African-American family that owned a home in times when so few did. As one of the neighbors put it tartly when discovering we were selling: "I'm African. We don't sell our land."

So I think about this as I look at the devastation of the Ninth Ward, for just one example, an area that has perhaps more African-American property owners than anyplace else in Louisiana. As I drove back and forth from the house I grew up in, carrying out pictures of my college graduation and my Latin notes from seventh grade, I heard a black woman on the radio describe how jarring it was to see the media describe her neighborhood as one riven by poverty and desperation. She was about to get her MBA, her brother already had his MBA, their extended family owned nine homes there, had insurance and owned cars in which they had fled for their lives. But it was the Ninth Ward; it was indeed being dubbed "poverty-stricken," "corrupt," "drug-ridden"; and politicians like Dennis Hastert were talking about bulldozing the entire area.

Race and class vied fiercely against each other—it's just poverty, poverty, poverty, according to the many commentators who were busy denying that the devastation had any link to race. I guess we don't like to talk about the way realtors take note of race—of how blacks "lower the property values" of the houses they move into, no matter how well kept. By the same token, when race was discussed, the black neighborhoods were almost romanticized as rickety, picturesque shantytowns destined for doom. The degree to which many of the black neighborhoods were also home to Louisiana's deep-rooted black working, middle and professional classes seemed lost entirely.

I began to wonder what might happen if I were not engaged in the relatively leisurely process of packing up my memories but was forced to run for my life. If it were not tragic enough to lose everything to the hurricane, it must have been many times more traumatizing to endure the chaotic evacuation that followed. It is hard to tell what's fact or fear in the witness accounts just yet, but the many descriptions of people being "sorted" in the shelters should give us pause. The elderly were taken from their families, the sick from their caretakers, newborns from their mothers and, because men were apparently segregated from women, husbands from wives, mothers from sons. I heard one unidentified authority saying that when people were evacuated to other states, they were not told where they were going so as to make them less unruly. But there were also accounts of white foreign nationals airlifted out "secretly" by National Guardsmen and warned not to go into the shelters because it was too dangerous for them.

On NPR a sociologist named Betty Hearn Morrow opined that it was less traumatic for people in distress to be grouped by their own kind. "That's just human nature," said Morrow.

Putting people into groups reinforces a sense of familiarity and security, so they should be relocated "according to their backgrounds." She gave an example of sorting people from Guatemala and Nicaragua and explained how that would help keep the peace.

My ears pricked up at this take on civil society; I wondered what "kind" I might appear to be in an evacuation. At 13, my son is almost six feet. If we were fleeing without any identification, would anyone believe he's a child? Would he be sorted with adults? Would he be separated from me? Would we be put on separate buses to unknown compass points? Would it really becalm me with a sense of "familiarity" to be penned up and marched off with a group of other black women of my "background"?

According to Mayor Bloomberg, the city of New York has been divided into grids in case of catastrophe. People would be ordered from their homes, or taken by force if necessary, and marshaled along preset routes to reception centers, where they would be identified by Social Security number and then relocated. I want to be a good citizen, part of the orderliness of a well-managed response to disaster. But with the images of New Orleans in mind, why on earth would any of us stream willingly toward chaos? It seems to me that one of the most pressing issues for the future is clarifying the precise protocols for evacuation. If it is true that families are to be broken up as a means of crowd control, then perhaps just a little public discussion is in order, no? And if it is true that white foreign nationals are a higher priority than black solid citizens, to what then do we pledge allegiance?

The Big Easy Dies Hard

by Christian Parenti

[from the September 26, 2005 issue]

THE EMPTY STREETS of this city present a vista of apocalyptic desolation: wind-ripped roofs, downed trees, smashed fast-food signs, dangling power lines, columns of dark smoke and everywhere heaps of garbage. On a lawn near the Ninth Ward three light brown mules, wandering the city alone, graze peacefully. In the sky above, helicopters drum the air. From the pale, empty stretches of elevated Interstate 10 one can look down on wide expanses of the city where homes are submerged in the flat, brackish floodwater. Strangely, the wind now is gritty and dry.

At first the city appears like a giant conceptual art installation, or the set of some archetypal cold-war disaster movie. But then comes evidence of what this really means: dazed refugees wade through the filthy water or push shopping carts down ravaged streets or wait silently in lines for evacuation. And every now and then there is the stench of abandoned corpses. Officials have no idea how many people are lost, trapped in the attics soon to be dead, or drowned and hidden in their homes.

Few can fathom the near-total lack of planning and coordination among local, state and federal authorities. "I been hearing about this is gonna happen for my whole life—how could they not have a plan?" says a man named Reginald Bell as he drops off extra candles to a neighbor.

On a side street in Algiers, on the flood-spared west bank, the corpse of a young black man in blue pants and white shirt lies rotting in the sun about ten feet from a chained-up health clinic. Swollen, greasy and oozing maggots, the dead man has become a symbol of official neglect. There are scores of uncollected corpses like this all over New Orleans.

"See, they just leave him here," says Malik Rahim, a community organizer who is spearheading a grassroots relief effort called the Green Cross. "He's been here almost five days, man." A colleague and I look down at the corpse dumbly. A police car rolls by. Another one stops, but the two white cops in it are dismissive. "We don't have the resources," says one.

"Their message to black people here is, Get out or die. You on your own," says Rahim, as the cops pull away.

The next day at the infamous convention center, where stunned refugees are being searched and then loaded onto outbound helicopters, a dozen ambulances sit waiting for orders. No rescues yet today, I am told. As for corpses, no one knows what the plan is.

Archie Haley, an emergency medical technician from Oak Grove, near the Arkansas border, squats as I scarf down a military MRE food ration; he explains that the major problem is "the large population of welfare-ized blacks who can't help themselves." My interlocutor is white like me, so he feels comfortable. "See, these people are the city's disease." His is an attitude that is far too common among officials here. Racism and incompetence seemed to merge to create a sluggish response. Despite all the troops, SWAT teams and out-of-town cops that have arrived since September 5, there's still little sign of a plan: On the ground, chaos reigns. Civilian volunteers are still doing many of the rescues; no one knows where to get water or MREs; the radio reports nothing of use.

By the Wednesday after Katrina hit, people here began to grow desperate as their stockpiles of supplies ran out. Survival looting, facilitated by the police, gave way to opportunistic rampaging and panic. "We grew more and more frightened each day because there was never any word from the government about emergency foods and water distribution, and we listened to the radio pretty regularly," says Mike Howell, a former academic, local peace activist and *Nation* reader I happened upon in a dark but open bar in the Bywater district. There is no power or water in this joint but somehow there is cold beer and free BBQ.

"All they kept saying was, Go to the Superdome, but we knew conditions over there were horrible, and we heard they weren't letting people back out who wanted to leave," says Howell.

Several SRO hotels, he says, have organized themselves into "communes" and do their survival looting in an organized and collectivist fashion. Everywhere one hears stories of mutual aid.

One of the most striking things about being in New Orleans is the number of people who outright refuse to leave. Howell calls them "the diehards." The mayor has ordered a mandatory evacuation, but the diehards, as well as thousands who live in dry, relatively unscathed areas, are poised to defy the order.

Out east on elevated I-10, above the dark, oily floodwaters of Elysian Fields, a man and his son are camped in a looted mail van. Two empty bottles of champagne sit on the dash; Black Power is spray-painted on the side. "We're bringing food and water back down in to the dogs. I got two of 'em still in the house." He points off east to roof-deep water.

At the far eastern edge of New Orleans, where the floodwater consumed I-10, a crew of rescuers from the state Department of Wildlife and Fisheries—biologists with boats—are getting ready to launch. They've been out here for days, bringing in water and bringing out the wounded, but as Clint Jeske explains, "A lot of people are in there just wading around, getting supplies and wading back in. They're living in half-flooded homes and they don't want to come out."

Nearby, in a sodden trailer park in the Chef Menteur Highway area, Paul Breaux sums it up thus: "I did two tours in Nam, went through the LA quake. I was a federal cop. I can deal with this. All I need is some resupply, some MREs and water." Breaux and three of his friends are camping outside their trailers; the water here had been four feet high but flowed out after a day. Why people should leave dry areas of the city is not at all clear. When pressed, some local officials say they might reconsider the order, which smacks of the incoherence and high-handedness that have characterized the whole evacuation. Refugees are loaded onto buses and just shipped away, not told where they're going or for how long. It's this sort of bad treatment that hardens people's resolve to stay.

By a levee on the west bank, school buses wait to load up. "I don't want to go far away, but I was in a boat with my disabled neighbor for five days eating nothing but potato chips and two gallons of water and some Gatorade," says a tall, skinny man named Lee from the totally submerged and oil-fouled St. Bernard Parish. "They just told us, Out," says another man, from the Algiers neighborhood, which has running water but no lights. The mayor has threatened to force people out and deny them food and water if they insist on staying.

Traditions of racism, exploitation and exclusion are visible in every aspect of this crisis. One also feels the repressive reflexes of the war on drugs and war on terror. Rather than work on rescue and cleanup with the mutual-aid networks, like the distribution efforts of Malik Rahim and his neighbor, the increasingly militarized local, state and federal agencies have defaulted to their worst bureaucratic instincts toward the dispossessed: silence, exclude, control and intimidate. Never mind why or toward what end.

FEMA:
Confederacy of Dunces

by Jon Elliston

[from the September 26, 2005 issue]

IN A WEEK full of evidence that the federal government is woefully unprepared to respond to natural disasters, the plaintive testimony of Aaron Broussard, president of Jefferson Parish, just outside New Orleans, stood out. "We have been abandoned by our own country," he told NBC's *Meet the Press*. Broussard recounted how local officials had been told "every single day, 'The cavalry's coming, the cavalry's coming, the cavalry's coming.' The cavalry's still not here yet," he said. "I've begun to hear the hoofs, and we're almost a week out."

It was an eerie echo of the aftermath of 1992's Hurricane Andrew, which killed twenty-three people and exposed deep weaknesses in federal emergency programs. "Where the hell is the cavalry?" the emergency manager of Dade County, Florida, famously pleaded several days after Andrew blew through.

After Andrew the cavalry got its act together. Reforms

engineered by President Clinton's Federal Emergency Management Agency director, James Lee Witt, won FEMA bipartisan praise throughout the 1990s. But by the time Hurricane Katrina roared into the Gulf, FEMA—the government entity that could have done the most to alleviate the crisis in the storm's wake—had been seriously hobbled by the Bush Administration. In 2002 FEMA was swallowed by the Department of Homeland Security—a move that the agency's current director, Michael Brown, promised would give the country a new, improved "FEMA on steroids." Instead, much of the agency's natural disaster work was sidelined in favor of antiterrorism programs.

"I am extremely concerned that the ability of our nation to prepare for and respond to disasters has been sharply eroded," Witt told Congress on March 24, 2004. The former director has urged that the agency be withdrawn from DHS—a proposal that's gaining traction in Congress following the Katrina meltdown.

While the Administration's push to privatize key services was draining the agency of some of its most experienced personnel, Bush appointed two FEMA directors with no substantive experience in disaster management. The first, Joe Allbaugh, was Bush's chief of staff in Texas. Allbaugh's handpicked successor, Brown, was an official with the International Arabian Horse Association before coming to FEMA. "Our professional staff are being systematically replaced by politically connected novices and contractors," Pleasant Mann—a seventeen-year FEMA veteran who was then head of the agency's government employees' union—complained to Congress last year. "A lot of the institutional knowledge is gone," Mann commented later. So is morale: In a February 2004 survey of FEMA personnel, 80 percent said FEMA had become "a poorer agency" under DHS.

That's not the worst of it. From its first months in office, the Bush Administration has chipped away at disaster mitigation programs designed to curb precisely the kind of damage now overwhelming Louisiana and neighboring states. Project Impact, a modest but influential mitigation program created by Witt in 1997, had spread to some 250 communities and all fifty states before it got the Bush budget ax in 2001. In Pascagoula, Mississippi, Project Impact was creating a database of structures in the local flood plain—crucial information that could have stemmed some of the havoc that city faces today. Such programs would have brought down the cost of repairing cities like Pascagoula: According to FEMA's own estimates, every dollar spent on mitigation saves roughly two dollars in disaster recovery costs.

No matter: In 2003 Congress approved a White House proposal to slash in half FEMA's Hazard Mitigation Grant Program—credited with saving an estimated $8.8 million in recovery costs in 1999 in three eastern North Carolina communities alone after Hurricane Floyd. The same year, the Bush Administration instituted a new program of mitigation grants awarded on a competitive basis. Again the experts warned against this approach, saying that less affluent and smaller communities would lose out on desperately needed funds.

One of the communities that lost out was Jefferson Parish. Last year FEMA turned down all three of its requests for flood-mitigation grants. At the time, Broussard's parish was home to more than 5,700 "repetitive loss structures"—buildings that had seen repeated flood damage and needed to be moved or elevated.

That missed opportunity in Jefferson Parish is one of many in the region that FEMA must now reckon with. It's all too easy to play Monday-morning quarterback amid the vast suffering along the Gulf Coast, but it's become all the more difficult to ignore the evidence that FEMA's ability to keep our country safe in the face of natural calamities, undermined by our Commander in Chief, is itself becoming a disaster.

Global Storm Warning

by Mark Hertsgaard

[from the October 17, 2005 issue]

H OW MANY KILLER hurricanes will it take before America gets serious about global warming? It's hard to imagine a more clear-cut wake-up call than Hurricane Katrina; environmentally speaking, it was nearly the perfect storm. In a single catastrophic event, it brought together the most urgent environmental problem of our time—global warming—with the most telling but least acknowledged environmental truth: When the bill for our collective behavior comes due, it is invariably the nonwhite, nonaffluent members of society who pay a disproportionate share. And who said Mother Nature has no sense of irony? Katrina (and then Rita) struck at a major production site for America's oil and natural gas—the two carbon-based fuels that, along with coal, help drive global warming.

What's more, Katrina's primary target already ranked as the most environmentally ravaged state in the union. Louisiana is home to "Cancer Alley," a 100-mile stretch between New Orleans and Baton Rouge that contains the greatest concentration of petrochemical factories in the United States. Pollution from those factories has punished nearby communities—again, mainly poor and black—for decades, as Steve Lerner documented in his recent book *Diamond*. This pollution has also drained into the Mississippi River, where it joins fertilizer and pesticide runoff from millions of acres of Midwestern farmland to flow into the Gulf of Mexico, creating a massive "dead zone" off the Louisiana coast—1,400 square miles of ocean floor as bereft of life as an Arizona desert. The dead zone would be smaller except that Louisiana, like America as a whole, has lost a third of its coastal wetlands to economic development. Wetlands filter out impurities, much as the liver does for the human body. They also perform a second vital ecosystem function, acting as buffers that absorb and diminish the giant waves that hurricanes generate before they strike inland. Louisiana's loss of wetlands helps explain why the floods Katrina unleashed ended up overrunning 466 chemical factories, thirty-one Superfund sites and 500 sewage treatment plants, according to the *Times-Picayune* and the *Houston Chronicle*, leaving behind a toxic soup whose long-term health effects are incalculable.

Despite these horrors some leading environmentalists see a potential silver lining in Katrina: They believe it may finally awaken the United States from its environmental complacency, especially about global warming. "Sea-level rise and increased storm intensity are no longer abstract, long-term issues but are associated with horrific pictures seen on television every evening," says Christopher Flavin, president of the Worldwatch Institute.

Yes, the Bush Administration and its right-wing allies will continue to deny that global warming exists and resist cutting carbon emissions. But global warming foot-draggers have succeeded in the past largely because the public was confused about whether the problem really existed. That confusion was encouraged by the mainstream media, which in the name of journalistic "balance" gave equal treatment to global warming skeptics and proponents alike, even though the skeptics represented a tiny fringe of scientific opinion and often were funded by companies with a financial interest in discrediting global warming. Katrina, however, may mark a turning point for the media as well as the public.

"THE REACTION HAS been more positive than any time in the sixteen years that I've been trying to make noise about global warming," says Bill McKibben, author of the 1989 classic *The End of Nature*. The day after Katrina hit, McKibben wrote an article for TomDispatch.com arguing that the devastation of New Orleans was, alas, only the first of many global warming disasters destined to strike in the twenty-first century. When McKibben appeared on radio shows to discuss the article, he says, "Everyone, and I mean everyone, who called in said, Thank heaven someone is saying this stuff, because it's what I'm thinking about all the time now."

"Had I said this stuff two years ago, the reactions would have ranged from skeptical to hostile, except for the liberal outlets," says Ross Gelbspan, whose Op-Ed article in the *Boston Globe* arguing that Katrina's "real name was global warming" led to forty-five media appearances. Gelbspan, who exposed industry funding of global warming skeptics in his book *The Heat Is On*, adds, "Even a couple of hostile, initially antagonistic right-wing talk-show hosts were drawn into the discussion—and their remarks turned from provocative to curious to sympathetic."

"There aren't many reporters left who believe the skeptics," says Phil Clapp, president of the National Environmental Trust. Clapp credits the joint statement issued by eleven of the world's national academies of science (including America's), before last June's meeting of the G-8 nations, declaring that global warming was a grave danger requiring immediate attention. "You may not have seen headlines screaming that Katrina was caused by global warming," Clapp adds, "but every reporter I've talked to has come to the position in their own mind that we have to prepare for global warming's effects."

But what journalists think in their own minds matters less than what they put on the air and in the papers. And given the gravity of the situation, screaming headlines are warranted. It's true that global warming can't be definitively blamed for one particular weather event; weather is the product of too many different factors to allow such specificity. Seizing on this fact, skeptics now trumpet scientific studies that portray Katrina as simply a manifestation of a natural long-term pattern in which first strong then weak hurricanes predominate. That pattern is real, but it doesn't invalidate global warming; the two trends can co-exist. The scientists at RealClimate.org offer a useful analogy: Imagine a set of dice loaded so that double sixes come up twice as often as normal. If the dice are then rolled and double sixes do come up, the loading may or may not be responsible for the result; after all, regular dice sometimes yield double sixes, too. All that's certain is that over time the frequency of double sixes will increase. Likewise, Katrina might have been

an extra-powerful hurricane even if humanity had never emit-
ted a single greenhouse gas. But over time, humanity's loading
of the climatic dice guarantees that there will be more killer
hurricanes like Katrina. We'd better get ready, and quickly.

Looting the Black Poor

by Earl Ofari Hutchinson

[from the September 26, 2005 issue]

FIVE DAYS BEFORE Hurricane Katrina struck, 100 people gathered at a local Catholic Church in eastern New Orleans. They were there to talk about the city's astronomically high poverty rate. This was not a dry gathering of academics, local and state officials, and business leaders. They were community residents, welfare recipients, ex-offenders and antipoverty activists. Most were black. Many did not have cars and had to take buses to get to the meeting. That wasn't unusual. Nearly one out of three city residents doesn't have a car. The participants felt they were in a race against time to combat the crisis—the poverty rate in New Orleans is more than double the national average. The city's poor had grown more numerous and more desperate than ever.

Whenever I have visited friends who live in neighborhoods away from the glitter of the French Quarter and other tourist spots, I've been struck by the dire poverty, the legions of home-less, the large number of abandoned and run-down buildings, the pockmarked streets and sidewalks. New Orleans is the classic tale of two cities: one showy, middle-class and white; the other poor, downtrodden and low-income black. It was a city that didn't wait for a disaster to happen; grinding poverty and neglect had already wreaked that disaster on thousands.

What happened after Katrina added to the misery was pre-dictable. Bush's bumbling and the bungling of FEMA turned relief efforts into a nightmare. That virtually guaranteed that some blacks out of criminal greed and others out of sheer des-peration and panic would take to the streets in an orgy of loot-ing and mayhem. It was equally predictable how some state and federal officials, and some in the media, would respond. They instantly branded the looters animals and thugs. Louisiana Governor Kathleen Blanco said soldiers should shoot to kill to restore order.

The same day Katrina struck, something else happened that also tells much about the Bush Administration's callous disre-gard for the poor. The Census Bureau released a report that found the number of poor Americans has jumped even higher since Bush took office in 2000, with blacks at the bottom of the eco-nomic totem pole. Bush's war and economic policies have added to their woes. His tax cuts redistributed billions to the rich and corporations. The Iraq War has drained billions from cash-starved job training, health and education programs. Increased dependence on foreign oil has driven gas and oil prices skyward. Corporate downsizing, outsourcing and industrial flight have further fueled America's poverty crisis, which has slammed young blacks, like those who ransacked stores in New Orleans, the hardest of all. Their unemployment rate is double and in some parts of the country triple that of white males.

During Bush's years, state and federal cutbacks in job training and skills programs, the brutal competition for low- and semi-skilled service and retail jobs from immigrants, and the refusal of many employers to hire those with criminal records have further hammered black communities and added to the depression-level unemployment figures among young blacks. The tale of poverty is more evident in the nearly 1 million blacks behind bars, the HIV/AIDS rampage in black communities, the sea of black homeless people and the raging drug and gang violence that rips apart many black communities.

The looting and poverty in New Orleans put an ugly public face on a crisis that Bush Administration policies have made worse. The millions in America who grow poorer and more desperate are bitter testament to those failures. The pity is that it took Bush's criminal incompetence and Mother Nature for the world to see that.

Class-ifying the Hurricane

by Adolph Reed, Jr.

[from the October 3, 2005 issue]

I WAS IN New Orleans visiting my mother and other relatives less than a week before Katrina hit. Even though we already had an eye on the approaching hurricane, I had no thought, when I boarded the plane to leave, that the city I've known all my life would never be the same again.

I don't have space or words to catalogue the horrors and outrages associated with the plight of New Orleans and its people. In any event, the basic story is now well-known, and we're entering the stage at which further details mainly feed the voyeuristic sentimentalism that will help the momentarily startled corporate news media retreat gracefully to their more familiar role as court heralds. The bigger picture will disappear in the minutiae of timelines and discrete actions.

What will be lost is the central point that the destruction was not an "act of God." Nor was it simply the product of incompetence, lack of empathy or cronyism. Those exist in abundance, to be sure, but they are symptoms, not ultimate causes. What happened in New Orleans is the culmination of twenty-five years of disparagement of any idea of public responsibility; of a concerted effort—led by the right but as part of a bipartisan consensus—to reduce government's functions to enhancing plunder by corporations and the wealthy and punishing everyone else, undermining any notion of social solidarity.

I know that some progressives believe this incident will mark a turning point in American politics. Perhaps, especially if gas prices continue to rise. I suspect, however, that this belief is only another version of the cargo cult that has pervaded the American left in different ways for a century: the wish for some magical intervention or technical fix that will substitute for organizing a broad popular base around a clearly articulated, alternative vision that responds to most people's pressing concerns. The greater likelihood is that within a month Democratic liberals will have smothered the political moment just as they've smothered every other opportunity we've had since Ronald Reagan's election. True, Nancy Pelosi and others finally began to bark at the Bush Administration's persisting homicidal negligence. But my hunch is that, as with Iran/contra, the theft of the 2000 election and the torrent of obvious lies that justified the war on Iraq, liberals' fear of seeming irresponsibly combative and their commitment to the primacy of corporate and investor-class interests will lead them to aid and abet the short-circuiting of whatever transformative potential this moment has.

This will also obscure the deeper reality that lies beneath the manifest racial disparities in vulnerability, treatment and outcome.

The abstract, moralizing patter about how and whether "race matters" or "the role of race" is appealing partly because it doesn't confront the roots of the bipartisan neoliberal policy regime. It's certainly true that George W. Bush and his minions are indifferent to, or contemptuous of, black Americans in general. They're contemptuous of anyone who is not part of the ruling class. Although Bush and his pals are no doubt small-minded bigots in many ways, the racial dimension stands out so strikingly in part because race is now the most familiar—and apparently for many progressives the most powerful—language of social justice. For roughly a generation it seemed reasonable to expect that defining inequalities in racial terms would provoke some remedial response from the federal government. But for quite some time race's force in national politics has been as a vehicle for reassuring whites that "public" equals some combination of "black," "poor" and "loser"; that cutting public spending is aimed at weaning a lazy black underclass off the dole or—in the supposedly benign, liberal Democratic version—teaching blacks "personal responsibility."

To paraphrase historian Barbara Fields, race is a language through which American capitalism's class contradictions are commonly expressed. Class will almost certainly turn out to be a better predictor than race of who was able to evacuate, who drowned, who was left to fester in the Superdome or on overpasses, who is stuck in shelters in Houston or Baton Rouge, or who is randomly dispersed to the four winds. I'm certain that class is also a better predictor than race of whose emotional attachments to place will be factored into plans for reconstructing the city.

Of course, in a case of devastation so vast as this, class position provides imperfect insulation. All my very well connected, petit-bourgeois family in New Orleans are now spread across Mississippi and south Louisiana with no hint of when they will return home or what they'll have to return to. Some may have lost their homes and all their belongings. But most of them evacuated before the storm. No one died or was in grave danger of dying; no one was left on an overpass, in the Superdome or at the convention center. They were fortunate but hardly unique among the city's black population, and class had everything to do with the terms of their survival.

Natural disasters can magnify existing patterns of inequality. The people who were swept aside or simply overlooked in this catastrophe were the same ones who were already swept aside in a model of urban revitalization that, in New Orleans as everywhere else, is predicated on their removal. Their presence is treated as an eyesore, a retardant of property values, proof by definition that the spaces they occupy are underutilized. And it's not simply because they're black. They embody another, more specific category, the equivalent of what used to be known, in the heyday of racial taxonomy, as a "sub-race." They are a population against which others—blacks as well as whites—measure their own civic worth. Those who were the greatest victims of the disaster were invisible in preparation and response, just as they were the largely invisible, low-wage props supporting the tourism industry's mythos of New Orleans as the city of constant carnival. They enter public discussion only as a problem to be rectified or contained, never as subjects of political action with their own voices and needs. White elites fret about how best to move them out of the way; black elites ventriloquize them and smooth their removal.

Race is too blunt an analytical tool even when inequality is expressed in glaring racial disparities. Its meanings are too vague. We can see already that the charges of racial insensitivity and neglect threaten to divert the focus of the Katrina outrage to a secondary debate about how Bush feels about blacks and whether the sources of the travesty visited upon poor New Orleanians were "color blind" or racist. Beyond that, a racial critique can lead nowhere except to demands for black participation in decision-making around reconstruction. But which black people? What plans? Reconstruction on what terms? I've seen too many black- and Latino-led municipal governments and housing authorities fuel real estate speculation with tax giveaways and zoning variances, rationalizing massive displacement of poor and other working-class people with sleight-of-hand about mixed-income occupancy and appeals to the sanctity of market forces.

The only hope we have for turning back the tide of this thuggish Administration's commitment to destroy every bit of social protection that's been won in the past century lies in finding ways to build a broad movement of the vast majority of us who are not part of the investor class. We have to be clear that what happened in New Orleans is an extreme and criminally tragic coming home to roost of the con that cutting public spending makes for a better society. It is a shocking foretaste of a future that many more of us will experience less dramatically, often quietly as individuals, as we lose pensions, union protection, access to healthcare and public education, Social Security, bankruptcy and tort protection, and as we are called upon to feed an endless war machine.

Bread, Roses, and the Flood

by Eric Foner

[from the October 3, 2005 issue]

T HIS TIME THE Bush Administration could not hide the dead bodies—or the walking wounded whose abandonment by American society began not in the hurricane's wake but many years earlier.

The only bright spot in this man-made disaster has been the wave of public outrage at the Administration's abject failure to provide aid to the most vulnerable. Indeed, it is hard to think of a time, other than at the height of the civil rights movement, when the plight of poor black Southerners so deeply stirred the conscience of the nation. Perhaps Hurricane Katrina will go down in history alongside Bull Connor's fire hoses in Birmingham and the Alabama Highway Patrol's nightsticks at Selma as a catalyst for a new national self-awareness regarding the unfinished struggle for racial justice.

But a better historical analogy, although not one that immediately springs to mind, may be the Lawrence, Massachusetts, strike of 1912, best known for giving the labor movement the slogan "bread and roses." Thousands of poor immigrant workers walked off their jobs in the city's giant woolen mills to protest a wage reduction. Bill Haywood, leader of the Industrial Workers of the World, who had been invited in to help direct the strike, devised a plan to send the workers' children to live with sympathetic families in other cities for the duration. The sight of the pale, emaciated children marching up Fifth Avenue transformed public opinion regarding the strike (leading the governor of Massachusetts to pressure the mill owners to accede to the workers' demands). More important, even though by 1912 the Progressive Era was well under way, the marches broadened public support for efforts to uplift the poor and placed the question of poverty, and the federal government's obligation to combat it, front and center in the presidential campaign of 1912.

"I have worked in the slums of New York," wrote Margaret Sanger, "but I have never found children who were so uniformly ill-nourished, ill-fed and ill-clothed." Today, as in 1912, the shameful (and growing) presence of poverty has been thrust from invisibility onto the center stage of national discussion. Let's hope the country finally awakens to the consequences of years of trickle-down economics, tax cuts for the rich, privatization of public responsibilities and the demonization of government and the poor.

Bohemia's Last Frontier

by Curtis Wilkie

[from the October 3, 2005 issue]

IF THE RESTORATION of New Orleans fails as miser-
ably as its rescue, the nation will have lost not only a
cultural treasure but an important enclave of progressive values and Democratic strength in the Deep South.

From the time French explorers claimed a clearing for a settlement along the massive river three centuries ago, New Orleans
existed as a place distinctly different from the rest of the country. There was nothing remotely Puritan about its early years. A
strong hint of the pagan could be smelled in the air, and in modern times the city became a refreshing detour off the Bible Belt-
way. While the rest of the region exercised piety, New Orleans
honored tolerance. In New Orleans, wine, women and song were
not synonymous with sin; gay people found refuge; and racially
mixed couples were acceptable at a time when there were laws
against miscegenation in neighboring states.

New Orleans was not without the racial tensions and urban problems that grip other American municipalities. Its public schools had deteriorated badly, presenting an image as shameful as its gang-infested housing projects. In the days since Katrina struck, the world has been exposed to New Orleans' saddest and seamiest side: the inequities that trapped the poor in neighborhoods vulnerable to flooding, the distrust that troubled relations between blacks and whites. New Orleans was always a poor place; that's why the blues resonated so clearly here. Yet a dogged live-and-let-live spirit helped the city transcend its difficulties and persevere as one of the last resorts for romantics.

Though a polyglot army of pirates and militiamen fought a famous battle a few miles down the river at the end of the War of 1812, New Orleans was not known to be bellicose like its sister cities in the South. The city surrendered without a fight at the beginning of the Civil War and endured its occupation with characteristic élan. Residents painted the visage of Union General Benjamin Butler on the bottom of their chamber pots and dumped the morning contents on the heads of Yankee soldiers from the same balconies where their descendants would fling Mardi Gras beads a century later. That was the extent of the resistance. New Orleans did not suffer from the hard-core Confederacy complex that still contributes to the South's conservatism. The city got over the war and went about the business of growing as a cosmopolitan port.

The city harbored slave markets in the first half of the nineteenth century. But even before Emancipation, New Orleans had a bourgeois class known as "free gentlemen of color." Many came from the Caribbean, spoke French and supported a network of educators, musicians and writers. After Reconstruction,

African-Americans and Creoles gained a foothold in New Orleans more rapidly than elsewhere in the South. Well before the Voting Rights Act of 1965, New Orleans blacks voted in large numbers, encouraged by the quirky populist regime of Huey Long, which controlled Louisiana during the Depression. The city's black society sent out two sons, Maynard Jackson and Andrew Young, who became mayors of Atlanta. By the mid-1970s the black majority had gained political supremacy in New Orleans as well, resulting in a succession of black mayors that continues to this day.

Disgruntled whites shuffled off to suburbs in Jefferson and St. Tammany parishes, and their departure left the city increasingly in the hands of blacks and whites unperturbed by racial fears. When David Duke, the wizard of a faction of the Ku Klux Klan, wound up in a runoff for governor of Louisiana in 1991, he was rejected overwhelmingly in New Orleans, where 87 percent voted for the eventual winner, Edwin Edwards. A year later the New Orleans vote provided Bill Clinton's margin of victory in Louisiana.

POLITICS IN NEW Orleans has been a byproduct of a way of life that grew out of the city's history. While much of the South was being settled by Calvinistic Scots-Irish immigrants, New Orleans developed as home for a mélange of ethnic backgrounds. French and Spanish flags flew over the city before the Louisiana Purchase in 1803. Slavery brought thousands from Africa. Then came the Irish and Italian laborers, German businessmen, Greek restaurateurs and merchants from the Middle East. By the beginning of the twentieth century New Orleans stood as a largely Roman Catholic island in a sea of Southern

Baptists. A strong, stable Jewish population provided more leavening. The Rev. Jimmy Swaggart might prosper down Airline Highway in Baton Rouge, but New Orleans was hostile territory for the tent revivalists and braying fundamentalist demagogues.

From its site in the deepest part of the South, New Orleans acted as an anti-Montgomery, offering an antithesis to the Southern stereotypes of redneck sheriffs, moonlight and magnolias. And it stubbornly resisted modern homogenization. New Orleans was a city of idiosyncrasies, sweeping from the palatial mansions along the St. Charles Avenue streetcar line to the rundown bungalows and shotgun houses in the working-class wards. Much of the architecture in the fabled French Quarter either reflected a Spanish influence or consisted of Creole cottages built in the Caribbean style. Despite its name, the Quarter was actually a residential neighborhood for Sicilian families for most of the past century, until it was discovered by artists and writers and antiestablishment characters such as Ruthie the Duck Girl, an elderly woman who kept a duck on a leash and cadged drinks in the corner bars.

In *Faulkner*, Joseph Blotner's biography, the author writes of how the aspiring Mississippi novelist and others were attracted to New Orleans after World War I. These "young artists in revolt and champions of the arts" were reacting, Blotner says, to H.L. Mencken's scornful 1917 essay "The Sahara of the Bozart." They felt Mencken's theory could be disproved in New Orleans.

The South, Mencken had claimed, was a cultural wasteland. "In all that gargantuan paradise of the fourth-rate," Mencken wrote, "there is not a single picture gallery worth going into, or a single orchestra capable of playing the nine symphonies of Beethoven, or a single opera-house, or a single theater devoted to decent plays, or a single monument that is worth looking at." Yet in New Orleans there were museums and orchestras and theaters. And the city nurtured writers, from Kate Chopin and Lillian Hellman to early Faulkner and Sherwood Anderson and, later, to Walker Percy and Richard Ford. Tennessee Williams called the French Quarter, the neighborhood he chose as his home, "the last frontier of Bohemia."

Before the storm New Orleans hosted two literary festivals: one linked to Faulkner, the other to Williams. The latter featured a contest for those who felt they could shout "Stella!" the loudest, a slightly refined example of street theater.

New Orleans could be raunchy. The striptease joints on Bourbon Street were tolerated for tourists' sake. But New Orleans preferred its own kind of spectacle, using the slightest excuse for a parade. St. Patrick's Day. St. Joseph's Day. Anybody's birthday. Hundreds of transvestites in outrageous drag marched every Labor Day in connection with an event called "Southern Decadence Weekend." To tweak the wealthy barons of Uptown, who bankrolled Mardi Gras through their private krewes—as they called the organizations responsible for the lavish carnival floats—commoners organized a rump parade called the "Krewe of Barkus." It involved several thousand hounds of all description parading through the French Quarter. Most famously, New Orleans turned a religious event into a bacchanal, spending the two weeks leading to Lent in revelry as boisterous as the celebrations in Venice and Rio de Janeiro. Lent, when it came, was not observed faithfully, abstinence not being in the New Orleans manner. Bars were open 24/7 and drinking permitted on the street. The city actually had an ordinance requiring bartenders to furnish plastic takeout containers known locally as Go-cups.

The celebrities in New Orleans were chefs, men and women who enjoyed a higher place in the city's pantheon than sports figures, political leaders or television personalities. New Orleanians talked about eating like Bostonians talk baseball. Visitors might have known about Antoine's and Commander's Palace, but locals knew Mandina's and Casamento's. The native cuisine was Creole—not to be confused with Cajun—and many of the ingredients came from the nearby Gulf. There was nothing bland about it. Even the lesser dishes were unique: the gigantic Muffuletta sandwich built with cold-cut salami and ground olives, the Po' Boys bulging with fried oysters, the Lucky Dogs that gave sustenance to millions of late-night drunks. (Oh, that Ignatius J. Reilly, the purveyor of Lucky Dogs in *A Confederacy of Dunces*, could see his city now.)

As much as New Orleans loved good food, it moved to music. Gospel. Folk. Funk. Blues. Rock 'n' roll. Jazz was born here, and when someone died here there was no better sendoff than a jazz funeral beginning with soulful dirges and ending in an explosion of colorful umbrellas and an upbeat version of "When the Saints Go Marching In." New Orleanians appreciated good music—Mencken be damned. They were connoisseurs of the improvisation or the backbeat. They knew that Kermit Ruffins blew his horn on Thursday night at an out-of-the-way spot in the Bywater section. That Aaron Neville sang carols a cappella on Christmas Eve at a church on Rampart Street.

Suddenly, the sounds are silent, the streets still, the people dispersed. Merriment has given way to lamentation, and no one knows when the good times will roll again.

Levee Town

by Alexander Cockburn

[from the October 3, 2005 issue]

WEATHER CAN WIPE out cities forever. It's what happened to America's first city, after all, as a visit to Chaco Canyon northeast of Gallup, New Mexico, attests. At the start of the thirteenth century it got hotter in that part of the world, and by the 1230s the Anasazi up and moved on. As the world now knows, weather need not have done New Orleans in. There are decades' worth of memos from engineers and contractors setting forth budgets for what it would take to build up those levees to withstand a Category 4 or Category 5 hurricane. The sum most recently nixed by Bush's OMB—$3 billion or so—is far less than what the Pentagon simply mislays every year.

New Orleans has bounced back before—though after the Civil War the city never really returned to its former glory. According to Lyle Saxon's *Fabulous New Orleans*, the last great social season came in 1859 with the largest receipts of produce, the heaviest and most profitable trade the city had ever done. The total river trade that year was valued at $289,565,000.

On April 24, 1862, New Orleans fell to the federal forces. Farragut's fleet broke through the blockade at the river's mouth. Soon thereafter federal ships passed the two forts below New Orleans. Tumult and confusion prevailed. To keep them out of enemy hands, 12,000 bales of cotton were rolled from the warehouses and set on fire. Warehouses crammed with tobacco and sugar were torched. Ships on the Mississippi, loaded with cotton, were burning too, and the sparks jumped to the steamboats. The Mississippi was aflame. As Saxon puts it, "gutters flowed molasses: sugar lay like drifted snow along the sidewalks." New Orleans had been sacked by its own people. The years of poverty and misery began.

With misery came masques, though it had actually been in 1857 that some young men from Mobile paraded during Mardi Gras as the Mystick Krewe of Comus, thus augmenting the traditional masked balls of the Creoles. In 1879 came the Twelfth Night Revelers. Then in 1872 Alexis Alexandrovich Romanov, brother to the Czar-apparent, was in town for carnival. They organized a parade for him, headed by a makeshift monarch, "Rex," a parody of the real thing.

In 1916 the first black krewe, the Zulu Social Aid and Pleasure Club, mimicked the mimicry of Rex by making the Zulu King's royal way the Basin Street Canal and his imperial float a skiff. As in the "life upside down" banquets of the Middle Ages, the parades and the masques parodied, or at least underlined, the real nature of things. As Errol Laborde, historian of Mardi Gras, describes it: "In the waning moments of the Carnival season, Rex and his queen greet Comus and his queen. Carnival custom recognizes Rex as the symbol of the people and Comus as the symbol of tradition and high society. It is more than symbolic that at the ceremonial conclusion of Carnival, Rex bows to Comus. In this act the people bow to society."

Hurricanes trump mime. In the wake of Katrina's onslaught, the people greeted Comus, taking the unpleasing form of Vice President Dick Cheney, with the finger and a four-letter word. But Comus will have the next laugh. The dearest wish of "society"—in its true guise as the expression of power and property—has always been to push Rex and his people off all potentially profitable real estate in the Crescent City, with the whole shoreline gentrified and the poor driven into hinterland ghettos. Thus were the better housing projects—such as Iberville and St. Thomas—scheduled for demolition nearly a generation ago, and the Superdome imposed upon what had been a thriving black neighborhood.

So, as Sonny Landreth puts it in his song "Levee Town," "Don't be surprised at who shows up, down in the Levee Town." As the waters recede poor neighborhoods will be swiftly red-tagged for the bulldozers. The "reconstruction" of New Orleans promises to be the first really big outing for the Kelo decision. Kelo? On June 23 the Supreme Court's liberals, plus Souter and Kennedy, decreed that between private property rights on the one side and big-time developers with city councils in their pockets on the other, the latter win every time, using the weapon of eminent domain in the furtherance of "public purpose." As Sandra Day O'Connor wrote in her dissent, "the specter of condemnation hangs over all property. Nothing is to prevent the State from replacing any Motel 6 with a Ritz-Carlton, any home with a shopping mall, or any farm with a factory." Or any black neighborhood with some simulacrum of the Garden District.

For most of its post-Civil War existence New Orleans was a pretty desperate city, despite its occasional boasts that it has the highest number of millionaires in America's fifty largest cities. I remember that in 1988, the year George Bush, Sr. accepted his nomination in the Superdome, some 26 percent of the city's inhabitants were below the poverty line and 50 percent could be classified as poor.

The scarcely suppressed class war in New Orleans was what gave the place, and its music, its edge. And why, at least until now, the Disneyfication of the core city could never quite be consummated. Barely had the hurricane passed before Speaker of the House Dennis Hastert caught the Republican mood nicely with his remarks that the city should be abandoned to the alligators, and Barbara Bush followed through with her considered view that for black people the Houston Astrodome represented the ne plus ultra in domestic amenities.

Music and street food are what anchored the city to its history. On any visit, you could hear blues singers whose active careers spanned six decades. Clarence "Gatemouth" Brown finally left us recently at 81. I heard him at JazzFest this spring, and though the Reaper had him by the elbow, Gatemouth still fired up the crowd: "Goodbye, I hate, I hate to leave you now, goodbye/Wish that I could help somehow/So long, so long for now, so long/I pray that I return, return to you some day/You pray that it shall be just that way/So long, so long for now, so long."

The Real Costs
of a Culture of Greed

by Robert Scheer

[First published in the *Los Angeles Times* and posted online on Thenation.com on September 6, 2005]

WHAT THE WORLD has witnessed this past week is an image of poverty and social disarray that tears away the affluent mask of the United States.

Instead of the much-celebrated American can-do machine that promises to bring freedom and prosperity to less fortunate people abroad, we have seen a callous official incompetence that puts even Third World rulers to shame. The well-reported litany of mistakes by the Bush Administration in failing to prevent and respond to Katrina's destruction grew longer with each hour's grim revelation from the streets of an apocalyptic New Orleans.

Yet the problem is much deeper. For half a century, free-market purists have to great effect denigrated the essential role that modern government performs as some terrible liberal plot. Thus, the symbolism of New Orleans' flooding is tragically apt: Franklin Roosevelt's New Deal and Louisiana Governor

Huey Long's ambitious populist reforms in the 1930s eased Louisiana out of feudalism and toward modernity; the Reagan Revolution and the callousness of both Bush Administrations have sent them back toward the abyss.

Now we have a President who wastes tax revenues in Iraq instead of protecting us at home. Levee improvements were deferred in recent years even after congressional approval, reportedly prompting EPA staffers to dub flooded New Orleans "Lake George."

None of this is an oversight, or simple incompetence. It is the result of a campaign by most Republicans and too many Democrats to systematically vilify the role of government in American life. Manipulative politicians have convinced lower- and middle-class whites that their own economic pains were caused by "quasi-socialist" government policies that aid only poor brown and black people—even as corporate profits and CEO salaries soared.

For decades we have seen social services that benefit every- one—education, community policing, public health, environ- mental protections and infrastructure repair, emergency services—in steady, steep decline in the face of tax cuts and ris- ing military spending. But it is a false savings; it will certainly cost exponentially more to save New Orleans than it would have to protect it in the first place.

And, although the wealthy can soften the blow of this national decline by sending their kids to private school, build- ing walls around their communities and checking into distant hotels in the face of approaching calamities, others, like the 150,000 people living below the poverty line in the Katrina damage area—one-third of whom are elderly—are left exposed.

Watching on television the stark vulnerability of a permanent underclass of African Americans living in New Orleans ghettos is terrifying. It should be remembered, however, that even when hurricanes are not threatening their lives and sanity, they live in rotting housing complexes, attend embarrassingly ill-equipped public schools and, lacking adequate police protection, are frequently terrorized by unemployed, uneducated young men.

In fact, rather than an anomaly, the public suffering of these desperate Americans is a symbol for a nation that is becoming progressively poorer under the leadership of the party of Big Business. As Katrina was making its devastating landfall, the U.S. Census Bureau released new figures that show that since 1999, the income of the poorest fifth of Americans has dropped 8.7 percent in inflation-adjusted dollars. Last year alone, 1.1 million were added to the 36 million already on the poverty rolls.

For those who have trouble with statistics, here's the shorthand: The rich have been getting richer and the poor have been getting, in the ripe populist language of Louisiana's legendary Long, the shaft.

These are people who have long since been abandoned to their fate. Despite the deep religiosity of the Gulf States and the United States in general, it is the gods of greed that seem to rule. Case in point: The crucial New Orleans marshland that absorbs excess water during storms has been greatly denuded by rampant commercial development allowed by a deregulation-crazy culture that favors a quick buck over long-term community benefits.

Given all this, it is no surprise that leaders, from the White House on down, haven't done right by the people of New

Orleans and the rest of the region, before and after what insurance companies insultingly call an "act of God."

Fact is, most of them, and especially our President, just don't care about the people who can't afford to attend political fundraisers or pay for high-priced lobbyists. No, these folks are supposed to be cruising on the rising tide of a booming, unregulated economy that "floats all boats."

They were left floating all right.

Found in the Flood

by Eric Alterman

[from the September 26, 2005 issue]

THE NEW ORLEANS flood produced a dizzying array of images both striking and shocking, but what was perhaps most unusual about them was the return to American television screens and newspaper front pages of poor people in a manner that was neither condescending nor condemnatory. A tone was set by the likes of Jason DeParle in the *New York Times*, who began his story like this: "The white people got out. Most of them, anyway. . . . it was mostly black people who were left behind. Poor black people, growing more hungry, sick and frightened by the hour as faraway officials counseled patience and warned that rescues take time." Wil Haygood in the *Washington Post* struck a similar tone (albeit buried on page A33): "To those who wonder why so many stayed behind when push came to water's mighty shove here, those who were trapped have a simple explanation: Their nickels and dimes and dollar bills simply didn't add up to stage a quick evacuation mission."

Beyond the confines of its much beloved tourist districts, New Orleans was a far poorer, blacker and more dangerous city than most Americans imagined. According to figures posted on The Progress Report, the Lower Ninth Ward, where the flooding was worst, is more than 98 percent black, with average annual household income below $27,500, not even half the national average, with a quarter of those earning less than $10,000. As Brian Wolshon, a consultant on the state's evacuation plan, told the *Times*, the city's evacuation plan paid little attention to its "low-mobility" population—the old, the sick and the poor with no cars or other way to get out of town.

It's impossible to tell why it was that so many TV news professionals, even the infamous media whores of cable news, caught the fever, unapologetically pointing to race and class as fundamental dimensions of the unfolding catastrophe. Perhaps they had no choice but to notice; perhaps their professional shame had grown unbearable during the years—even the post-9/11 years—of covering to death every missing little blue-eyed, blond white girl; perhaps, caught inside the tragedy, their human spirits collided with their professional selves. No matter the reason, it was a sight to behold.

In an interview with House majority leader Tom DeLay, African-American MSNBC anchor Lester Holt asked, "People are now beginning to voice what we've all been seeing with our own eyes—the majority of people left in New Orleans are black, they are poor, they are the underbelly of society. When you look at this, what does this say about where we are as a country and where our government is in terms of how it views the people of this country?" When DeLay responded with the usual right-wing nonsense—"We're doing a wonderful job, and we are an incredibly compassionate people"—Holt refused to back off. "Those people at the Superdome, those people at the convention center. They're largely black, and they're largely poor, and they're largely left behind. What does that say about our country right now and how it treats its citizens?" MSNBC also showed Condoleezza Rice looking no less out-to-lunch addressing the cameras than she had the day before, shopping for shoes. "You've spoken very eloquently around the world about growing up as an African-American in the South," she was pointedly asked. "Are you concerned now that at least the impression is going to exist in this country and abroad that some of the relief has been affected by the race and class of the people most affected?" The Secretary of State shamed her heritage as well as her PhD with the idiotic response, "That Americans would somehow in a color-affected way decide who to help and who not to help, I just don't believe it."

While MSNBC played far above its usual batting average, it was CNN whose aggressive and impassioned reporting provided the biggest surprise and offered perhaps the finest coverage in the network's history. Chris Lawrence described "babies 3, 4, 5 months old, living in these horrible conditions. . . . These people are being forced to live like animals." Paula Zahn grilled the hapless Bush crony Michael Brown, who pretends to direct FEMA. "And finally tonight, sir," she demanded, "you said earlier today that part of the blame for the—what you think will be an—enormous death toll in New Orleans rests with the people who did not evacuate the city, who didn't heed the warnings. Is that fair, to blame the victims, many of whom tell us they had no way out, they had no cars of their own, and that public assistance wasn't provided to get them out of the city?" Jack Cafferty's commentaries were also impressive: smart, gutsy and focused on the issues of race, class, poverty, federal incompetence and the cost to the victims of having 40 percent of the National Guard away at war.

Yet in the media's Bush propaganda wing, Fox was still Fox. Bill O'Reilly, deaf and blind to the obvious class implications of the pre-flood exodus, speculated, "A lot of the people who stayed wanted to do this destruction" and wondered why "looters" were not being shot on sight. Indeed, aside from the surprisingly passionate Shephard Smith, much of Fox's reporting could have been datelined "Neverland." Neil Cavuto brought in Rick Warren, author of *The Purpose-Driven Life*, to advise those who'd lost everything to "play it down and pray it up." Fred Barnes complained that those in need had purposely bilked the taxpayers with their cavalier choice of domiciles. "They know they're going to flood. And when these things happen, they want the taxpayers all over the country to pay, and they do." Charles Krauthammer joshed back, "It's a bit unseemly to talk about cutting off aid to these people while the hurricane is still roaring through Mississippi. But let's give it a try," proceeding to needle Barnes about his own summer house. Together with Brit Hume, the Fox pundits laughed about the rain damage to the cover of the Barnes family swimming pool.

Yes, it was a regular laugh-riot over at Fox. But for once, the rest of the media did not follow them into the sewer and instead gave their faux-news phonies a chance to see how real journalists do the job.

The Disaster President

by The Editors

[from the September 26, 2005 issue]

A s THE FOURTH anniversary of September 11 approached, Americans were increasingly disquieted by the costly quagmire in Iraq, rising gas prices and an economy that benefits only CEOs. Then the destruction visited upon the Gulf Coast by Hurricane Katrina, and the grossly negligent government response to the flooding that followed, exposed the full scope of George W. Bush's misrule. The failures were so outrageous they roused even our embedded media from its slumbers.

But the incompetence revealed by the response to the hurricane is deep-rooted, and can be traced to the twenty-five-year project, begun in the Reagan era, of discrediting government, "starving the beast" of resources and exalting private markets and faith-based charities. Tax cuts for the wealthy and Congressional corruption have drained government of the imagination and resources to address human needs. Katrina has brutally exposed Americans to the costs of this folly.

The spending squeeze that delayed the strengthening of the levees in New Orleans—despite repeated warnings from experts—reflects this Administration's skewed priorities: money for war and occupation in Iraq but not for protection of life at home. With one-third of the troops and half the equipment of the Louisiana and Mississippi National Guard in Iraq, Americans saw stark evidence of the domestic price of the war this President has chosen to fight on credit. And the chilling scenes of calamity visited on the most vulnerable exposed to the world America's reality: a country ever more divided by race and class.

The Gulf Coast looked, said Bush, like it had been hit with "the worst kind of weapon." The President is right, responded Representative Dennis Kucinich. "Indifference is a weapon of mass destruction." While most of the affluent of New Orleans left by car or plane, the poor had no way out. They were told to go to the Superdome and convention center, where—unbelievably—there were inadequate supplies of food and water, no electricity, befouled sanitation facilities and no police protection. When it came time to rescue and relocate the displaced, the Bush Administration placed the onus on state and local officials and called on citizens to give to charities. But faith-based disaster relief is no substitute for an effective, organized, rapid government response.

Since New Orleans is a major center of oil imports and refining, Katrina roiled already tight energy markets. Gas companies, wallowing in record profits, took the occasion to gouge Americans at the pump. The companies' rapacity and the country's vulnerability are direct results of Bush's Big Oil energy policy, his failure to lead a drive for energy independence by investing in conservation and in renewable and diverse energy sources. Instead of calling for an excess-profits tax on oil companies to help pay for the rebuilding, Bush immediately asserted that no tax increase was necessary.

The staggering incompetence of the Department of Homeland Security—which disregarded its own forecasts—exposed this Administration's glaring failure to prepare for emergencies after September 11. In the chaotic reorganization of DHS, the powers of FEMA, the agency in charge of natural disasters, were weakened and its budget slashed.

Now, in the wake of Katrina, America must begin rebuilding from the ruins caused by nature and policy. A massive public works project is imperative for New Orleans and neighboring communities, one with affordable housing and adequate planning for flood and storm protection. We must restore the wetlands and barrier islands that have been degraded by canals and levees.

The disaster requires a thorough investigation into what went wrong, by an independent commission with subpoena power. It should also lead now-furious Americans to re-examine a generation of backward priorities. The debate about the role of government in the service of public good has been reopened. The hurricane revealed not only the desperate poverty of the region's African-American population but also the poverty of our federal policies. For too long our leaders have abandoned our cities, our poor, our public infrastructure. We need a government dedicated to serving the unemployed, the ill fed and the ill housed. It's time to end the dismantling and begin the rebuilding.

There is nothing in George Bush's policies or actions to suggest that his Administration has the leadership or the values for the task. To recover from this government's follies, Americans need a relocation and reclamation project in Washington, D.C., in addition to the massive one beginning in Katrina's wake.

TWO

The Looting of New Orleans

Purging the Poor

by Naomi Klein

[from the October 10, 2005 issue]

OUTSIDE THE 2,000-BED temporary shelter in Baton Rouge's River Center, a Church of Scientology band is performing a version of Bill Withers's classic "Use Me"—a refreshingly honest choice. "If it feels this good getting used," the Scientology singer belts out, "just keep on using me until you use me up."

Ten-year-old Nyler, lying facedown on a massage table, has pretty much the same attitude. She is not quite sure why the nice lady in the yellow SCIENTOLOGY VOLUNTEER MINISTER T-shirt wants to rub her back, but "it feels so good," she tells me, so who really cares? I ask Nyler if this is her first massage. "Assist!" hisses the volunteer minister, correcting my Scientology lingo. Nyler shakes her head no; since fleeing New Orleans after a tree fell on her house, she has visited this tent many times, becoming something of an assist-aholic. "I have nerves," she explains in a blissed-out massage voice. "I have what you call nervousness."

Wearing a donated pink T-shirt with an age-inappropriate slogan ("It's the hidden little Tiki spot where the island boys are hot, hot, hot"), Nyler tells me what she is nervous about. "I think New Orleans might not ever get fixed back." "Why not?" I ask, a little surprised to be discussing reconstruction politics with a preteen in pigtails. "Because the people who know how to fix broken houses are all gone."

I don't have the heart to tell Nyler that I suspect she is on to something; that many of the African-American workers from her neighborhood may never be welcomed back to rebuild their city. An hour earlier I had interviewed New Orleans' top corporate lobbyist, Mark Drennen. As president and CEO of Greater New Orleans Inc., Drennen was in an expansive mood, pumped up by signs from Washington that the corporations he represents—everything from Chevron to Liberty Bank to Coca-Cola—were about to receive a package of tax breaks, subsidies and relaxed regulations so generous it would make the job of a lobbyist virtually obsolete.

Listening to Drennen enthuse about the opportunities opened up by the storm, I was struck by his reference to African-Americans in New Orleans as "the minority community." At 67 percent of the population, they are in fact the clear majority, while whites like Drennen make up just 27 percent. It was no doubt a simple verbal slip, but I couldn't help feeling that it was also a glimpse into the desired demographics of the new-and-improved city being imagined by its white elite, one that won't have much room for Nyler or her neighbors who know how to fix houses. "I honestly don't know and I don't think anyone knows how they are going to fit in," Drennen said of the city's unemployed.

New Orleans is already displaying signs of a demographic shift so dramatic that some evacuees describe it as "ethnic cleansing." Before Mayor Ray Nagin called for a second evacuation, the people streaming back into dry areas were mostly white, while those with no homes to return to are overwhelmingly black. This, we are assured, is not a conspiracy; it's simple geography—a reflection of the fact that wealth in New Orleans buys altitude. That means that the driest areas are the whitest (the French Quarter is 90 percent white; the Garden District, 89 percent; Audubon, 86 percent; neighboring Jefferson Parish, where people were also allowed to return, 65 percent). Some dry areas, like Algiers, did have large low-income African-American populations before the storm, but in all the billions for reconstruction, there is no budget for transportation back from the far-flung shelters where those residents ended up. So even when resettlement is permitted, many may not be able to return.

As for the hundreds of thousands of residents whose low-lying homes and housing projects were destroyed by the flood, Drennen points out that many of those neighborhoods were dysfunctional to begin with. He says the city now has an opportunity for "twenty-first-century thinking": Rather than rebuild ghettos, New Orleans should be resettled with "mixed income" housing, with rich and poor, black and white living side by side.

What Drennen doesn't say is that this kind of urban integration could happen tomorrow, on a massive scale. Roughly 70,000 of New Orleans' poorest homeless evacuees could move back to the city alongside returning white homeowners, without a single new structure being built. Take the Lower Garden District, where Drennen himself lives. It has a surprisingly high vacancy rate—17.4 percent, according to the 2000 Census. At that time 702 housing units stood vacant, and since the market hasn't improved and the district was barely flooded, they are presumably still there and still vacant. It's much the same in the other dry areas: With landlords preferring to board up apartments rather than lower rents, the French Quarter has been half-empty for years, with a vacancy rate of 37 percent.

The citywide numbers are staggering: In the areas that sustained only minor damage and are on the mayor's repopulation list, there are at least 11,600 empty apartments and houses. If Jefferson Parish is included, that number soars to 23,270. With three people in each unit, that means homes could be found for roughly 70,000 evacuees. With the number of permanently homeless city residents estimated at 200,000, that's a significant dent in the housing crisis. And it's doable. Democratic Representative Sheila Jackson Lee, whose Houston district includes some 150,000 Katrina evacuees, says there are ways to convert vacant apartments into affordable or free housing. After passing an ordinance, cities could issue Section 8 certificates, covering rent until evacuees find jobs. Jackson Lee says she plans to introduce legislation that will call for federal funds to be spent on precisely such rental vouchers. "If opportunity exists to create viable housing options," she says, "they should be explored."

Malcolm Suber, a longtime New Orleans community activist, was shocked to learn that thousands of livable homes were sitting empty. "If there are empty houses in the city," he says, "then working-class and poor people should be able to live in them." According to Suber, taking over vacant units would do more than provide much-needed immediate shelter: It would move the poor back into the city, preventing the key decisions about its future—like whether to turn the Ninth Ward into marshland or how to rebuild Charity Hospital—from being made exclusively by those who can afford land on high ground. "We have the right to fully participate in the reconstruction of our city," Suber says. "And that can only happen if we are back inside." But he concedes that it will be a fight: The old-line families in Audubon and the Garden District may pay lip service to "mixed income" housing, "but the Bourbons uptown would have a conniption if a Section 8 tenant moved in next door. It will certainly be interesting."

Equally interesting will be the response from the Bush Administration. So far, the only plan for homeless residents to move back to New Orleans is Bush's bizarre Urban Homesteading Act. In his speech from the French Quarter, Bush made no mention of the neighborhood's roughly 1,700 unrented apartments and instead proposed holding a lottery to hand out plots of federal land to flood victims, who could build homes on them. But it will take months (at least) before new houses are built, and many of the poorest residents won't be able to carry the mortgage, no matter how subsidized. Besides, it barely touches the need: The Administration estimates that in New Orleans there is land for only 1,000 "homesteaders."

The truth is that the White House's determination to turn renters into mortgage payers is less about solving Louisiana's housing crisis than indulging an ideological obsession with building a radically privatized "ownership society." It's an obsession that has already come to grip the entire disaster zone, with emergency relief provided by the Red Cross and Wal-Mart and reconstruction contracts handed out to Bechtel, Fluor, Halliburton and Shaw—the same gang that spent the past three years getting paid billions while failing to bring Iraq's essential services to prewar levels. "Reconstruction," whether in Baghdad or New Orleans, has become shorthand for a massive uninterrupted transfer of wealth from public to private hands, whether in the form of direct "cost plus" government contracts or by auctioning off new sectors of the state to corporations.

This vision was laid out in uniquely undisguised form during a meeting at the Heritage Foundation's Washington headquarters on September 13. Present were members of the House Republican Study Committee, a caucus of more than 100 conservative lawmakers headed by Indiana Congressman Mike Pence. The group compiled a list of thirty-two "Pro-Free-Market Ideas for Responding to Hurricane Katrina and High Gas Prices," including school vouchers, repealing environmental regulations and "drilling in the Arctic National Wildlife Refuge." Admittedly, it seems farfetched that these would be adopted as relief for the needy victims of an eviscerated public sector. Until you read the first three items: "Automatically suspend Davis-Bacon prevailing wage laws in disaster areas"; "Make the entire affected area a flat-tax free-enterprise zone"; and "Make the entire region an economic competitiveness zone (comprehensive tax incentives and waiving of regulations)." All are poised to become law or have already been adopted by presidential decree.

In their own way the list-makers at Heritage are not unlike the 500 Scientology volunteer ministers currently deployed to shelters across Louisiana. "We literally followed the hurricane,"

David Holt, a church supervisor, told me. When I asked him why, he pointed to a yellow banner that read, SOMETHING CAN BE DONE ABOUT IT. I asked him what "it" was and he said "everything."

So it is with the neocon true believers: Their "Katrina relief" policies are the same ones trotted out for every problem, but nothing energizes them like a good disaster. As Bush says, lands swept clean are "opportunity zones," a chance to do some recruiting, advance the faith, even rewrite the rules from scratch. But that, of course, will take some massaging—I mean assisting.

Doing the Math

by Naomi Klein and Aaron Maté

[Sidebar to "Purging the Poor," posted online on September 20, 2005]

Here's how we identified more than 11,000 empty, rentable homes in New Orleans:

On September 15, New Orleans Mayor Ray Nagin announced that residents in areas with the following zip codes would be allowed to return to their neighborhoods, most of which escaped serious damage from Hurricane Katrina: 70131, 70114, 70118, 70115, 70130, 70113, 70112 and 70116. (He has since temporarily suspended the repopulation plan.)

At least six of New Orleans' twelve districts have neighborhoods that fall within these zip codes. The Greater New Orleans Community Data Center provides the latest Census data for each of the city's seventy-three neighborhoods. Looking only at those that fall within the zip codes deemed habitable by the mayor, we calculated each neighborhood's number of vacant housing units by multiplying that neighborhood's total number of housing units by its vacancy rate:

Available Housing Units by Neighborhood
Neighborhood Vacant Housing Units
Central Business District 252
French Quarter 1,736
Uptown/Carrollton 2,383
Algiers 2,713
New Aurora/ English Turn 115
Central City/Garden District 4,418

Adding them all up equals 11,617 vacant housing units in New Orleans' dry zones. When we include neighboring Jefferson Parish to the west of the city, the total jumps to 23,267.

Some neighborhoods fall within more than one zip code area. In those cases where a neighborhood included on the mayor's list also has a Zip Code that is not, that neighborhood was excluded in its entirety.

The number of available homes in the New Orleans area may therefore be higher than we have estimated. One exception was made with the Central City neighborhood in the Central/Garden District.

This neighborhood shares four zip codes, one of which was not on the mayor's list. But this zone represents about one-quarter of the area, and its inclusion is more than offset by the many other vacant homes in those other half-flooded, half-dry neighborhoods that we have left out of our total.

GOP Opportunity Zone

[Sidebar to "Purging the Poor," posted online on September 23, 2005]

THIS IS A list of "Pro-Free-Market Ideas for Responding to Hurricane Katrina and High Gas Prices," circulated by the House Republican Study Committee. Attributions included where available.

- Automatically suspend Davis-Bacon prevailing wage laws in disaster areas. (Reps. Marilyn Musgrave, Colorado, Tom Feeney, Florida, Jeff Flake, Arizona)
- Make the entire affected area a flat-tax free-enterprise zone. (Rep. Paul Ryan, Wisconsin)
- Make the entire region an economic competitiveness zone (comprehensive tax incentives and waiving of regulations). (Rep. Todd Tiahrt, Kansas)
- Immediate, first-year business expensing in lieu of depreciation for all assets, both personal property and structures (buildings) in the affected areas.

- Allow net operating loss carry-backs for affected residents and businesses going back as many years as is needed to actualize the NOL.
- For residents and businesses located or investing in the affected area, their 2005 and 2006 capital gains and dividends rate should be zero.
- Individuals in the affected area should have a Section 911 (overseas earned income) exclusion that is uncapped.
- Waive the death tax for any deaths in the affected area between August 20, 2005–December 31, 2005.
- Provide limited liability protection for construction contractors who voluntarily provide services or equipment before a government contract is finalized. (Rep. Gary Miller, California, Rep. Tom Cole, Oklahoma)
- Repeal or waive restrictive environmental regulations, such as NEPA, that hamper rebuilding. (Heritage Foundation)
- Waive penalties for early withdrawals from tax-advantaged savings (like IRAs and 401k accounts). (Heritage Foundation)
- Eliminate any regulatory barriers and other disincentives that block faith-based and other charitable organizations from engaging in the recovery and reconstruction process. (Orthodox Union, Heritage Foundation)
- Increase the amount of rehabilitation tax credits by 30 percent in census tracts where the greatest poverty exists, and for smaller projects where raising capital for reconstruction is the most difficult, and where there is the most critical need for housing and neighborhood reinvestment. (Rep. Phil English, Pennsylvania)

- Allow non-itemizers to deduct charitable contributions to disaster relief. (Rep. Ron Paul, Texas)
- Give school-choice vouchers for displaced children. (Rep. Ted Poe, Texas)
- Provide tax (and other such) incentives to lenders if they provide funding for school and other construction.
- Reduce, suspend, or eliminate tariffs on Canadian lumber, Mexican cement, and other materials used for new construction.
- Permit an additional advance refunding for all governmental bonds issued by or on the behalf of entities contained in the disaster area as declared by the president.
- Eliminate the volume cap for private-activity bonds in the disaster area and permit the use of private-activity bonds for all transportation-related infrastructure in the disaster area.
- Eliminate the income and home price limitation for mortgages funded by tax-exempt mortgage revenue bonds for a five-year period.
- Allow a non-profit corporation to issue tax-credit bonds—which provide a return in the form of a federal tax credit—and allocate the proceeds for school rehabilitation and reconstruction.
- Streamline the environmental hurdles to building new oil refineries. (Rep. John Shadegg, Arizona)
- Make it easier for small refineries to increase capacity. (Kansas's Tiahrt)
- Allow more offshore oil drilling. (Texas's Poe)
- Pay the royalties for new offshore oil drilling to the local governments nearest to shore. (Rep. Dana Rohrabacher, California)

- Allow drilling in the Arctic National Wildlife Refuge.
- Temporarily suspend the gas tax. (Arizona's John Shadegg)
- Permanently reduce the gas tax.
- Waive or repeal gas formulation (e.g. oxygenation) requirements under the Clean Air Act and related regulations. (Heritage Foundation)
- Encourage the production of renewable fuels (biodiesel, ethanol).
- Encourage private-market projects to recover usable energy from oil shale.
- Strengthen the existing investment tax credit for Enhanced Oil Recovery (using modern technology improvements to extract oil from previously unavailable sources) in section 43 of the IRS Code.

Source: House Republican Study Committee

Blackwater Down

by Jeremy Scahill

[from the October 10, 2005 issue]

THE MEN FROM Blackwater USA arrived in New Orleans right after Katrina hit. The company known for its private security work guarding senior U.S. diplomats in Iraq beat the federal government and most aid organizations to the scene in another devastated Gulf, deploying about 150 armed private troops dressed in full battle gear. Officially, the company boasted of its forces "join[ing] the hurricane relief effort." But its men on the ground told a different story.

Some patrolled the streets in SUVs with tinted windows and the Blackwater logo splashed on the back; others sped around the French Quarter in an unmarked car with no license plates. They congregated on the corner of St. James and Bourbon in front of a bar called 711, where Blackwater was establishing a makeshift headquarters. From the balcony above the bar, several Blackwater guys cleared out what had apparently been someone's apartment. They threw mattresses, clothes, shoes and other household items from the balcony to the street below. They draped an American flag from the balcony's railing. More than a dozen troops from the 82nd Airborne Division stood in formation on the street watching the action.

Armed men shuffled in and out of the building as a handful told stories of their past experiences in Iraq. "I worked the security detail of both Bremer and Negroponte," said one of the Blackwater guys, referring to the former head of the U.S. occupation, L. Paul Bremer, and former U.S. Ambassador to Iraq John Negroponte. Another complained, while talking on his cell phone, that he was getting only $350 a day plus his per diem. "When they told me New Orleans, I said, 'What country is that in?' " he said. He wore his company ID around his neck in a case with the phrase Operation Iraqi Freedom printed on it.

In an hourlong conversation I had with four Blackwater men, they characterized their work in New Orleans as "securing neighborhoods" and "confronting criminals." They all carried automatic assault weapons and had guns strapped to their legs. Their flak jackets were covered with pouches for extra ammunition.

When asked what authority they were operating under, one guy said, "We're on contract with the Department of Homeland Security." Then, pointing to one of his comrades, he said, "He was even deputized by the governor of the state of Louisiana. We can make arrests and use lethal force if we deem it necessary." The man then held up the gold Louisiana law enforcement badge he wore around his neck. Blackwater spokesperson Anne Duke also said the company has a letter from Louisiana officials authorizing its forces to carry loaded weapons.

"This vigilantism demonstrates the utter breakdown of the government," says Michael Ratner, president of the Center for Constitutional Rights. "These private security forces have behaved brutally, with impunity, in Iraq. To have them now on the streets of New Orleans is frightening and possibly illegal."

Blackwater is not alone. As business leaders and government officials talk openly of changing the demographics of what was one of the most culturally vibrant of America's cities, mercenaries from companies like DynCorp, Intercon, American Security Group, Blackhawk, Wackenhut and an Israeli company called Instinctive Shooting International (ISI) are fanning out to guard private businesses and homes, as well as government projects and institutions. Within two weeks of the hurricane, the number of private security companies registered in Louisiana jumped from 185 to 235. Some, like Blackwater, are under federal contract. Others have been hired by the wealthy elite, like F. Patrick Quinn III, who brought in private security to guard his $3 million private estate and his luxury hotels, which are under consideration for a lucrative federal contract to house FEMA workers.

A possibly deadly incident involving Quinn's hired guns underscores the dangers of private forces policing American streets. On his second night in New Orleans, Quinn's security chief, Michael Montgomery, who said he worked for an Alabama company called Bodyguard and Tactical Security (BATS), was with a heavily armed security detail en route to pick up one of Quinn's associates and escort him through the chaotic city. Montgomery told me they came under fire from "black gangbangers" on an overpass near the poor Ninth Ward neighborhood. "At the time, I was on the phone with my business partner," he recalls. "I dropped the phone and returned fire."

Montgomery says he and his men were armed with AR-15s and Glocks and that they unleashed a barrage of bullets in the general direction of the alleged shooters on the overpass. "After that, all I heard was moaning and screaming, and the shooting stopped. That was it. Enough said."

Then, Montgomery says, "the Army showed up, yelling at us and thinking we were the enemy. We explained to them that we were security. I told them what had happened and they didn't even care. They just left." Five minutes later, Montgomery says, Louisiana state troopers arrived on the scene, inquired about the incident and then asked him for directions on "how they could get out of the city." Montgomery says that no one ever asked him for any details of the incident and no report was ever made. "One thing about security," Montgomery says, "is that we all coordinate with each other—one family." That co-ordination doesn't include the offices of the Secretaries of State in Louisiana and Alabama, which have no record of a BATS company.

A few miles away from the French Quarter, another wealthy New Orleans businessman, James Reiss, who serves in Mayor Ray Nagin's administration as chairman of the city's Regional Transit Authority, brought in some heavy guns to guard the elite gated community of Audubon Place: Israeli mercenaries dressed in black and armed with M-16s. Two Israelis patrolling the gates outside Audubon told me they had served as professional soldiers in the Israeli military, and one boasted of having participated in the invasion of Lebanon. "We have been fighting the Palestinians all day, every day, our whole lives," one of them tells me. "Here in New Orleans, we are not guarding from terrorists." Then, tapping on his machine gun, he says, "Most Americans, when they see these things, that's enough to scare them."

The men work for ISI, which describes its employees as "veterans of the Israeli special task forces from the following Israeli government bodies: Israel Defense Force (IDF), Israel National Police Counter Terrorism units, Instructors of Israel National Police Counter Terrorism units, General Security Service (GSS or 'Shin Beit'), Other restricted intelligence agencies." The company was formed in 1993. Its Web site profile says: "Our up-to-date services meet the challenging needs for Homeland Security preparedness and overseas combat procedures and readiness. ISI is currently an approved vendor by the U.S. Government to supply Homeland Security services."

Unlike ISI or BATS, Blackwater is operating under a federal contract to provide 164 armed guards for FEMA reconstruction projects in Louisiana. That contract was announced just days after Homeland Security Department spokesperson Russ Knocke told the *Washington Post* he knew of no federal plans to hire Blackwater or other private security firms. "We believe we've got the right mix of personnel in law enforcement for the federal government to meet the demands of public safety," he said. Before the contract was announced, the Blackwater men told me, they were already on contract with DHS and they were sleeping in camps organized by the federal agency.

One might ask, given the enormous presence in New Orleans of National Guard, U.S. Army, U.S. Border Patrol, local police from around the country and practically every other government agency with badges, why private security companies are needed, particularly to guard federal projects. "It strikes me . . . that that may not be the best use of money," said Illinois Senator Barack Obama.

Blackwater's success in procuring federal contracts could well be explained by major-league contributions and family connections to the GOP. According to election records, Blackwater's CEO and co-founder, billionaire Erik Prince, has given tens of thousands to Republicans, including more than $80,000 to the Republican National Committee the month before Bush's victory in 2000. In June 2005, he gave $2,100 to Senator Rick Santorum's re-election campaign. He has also given to House majority leader Tom DeLay and a slew of other Republican candidates, including Bush/Cheney in 2004. As a young man, Prince interned with President George H.W. Bush, though he complained at the time that he "saw a lot of things I didn't agree with—homosexual groups being invited in, the budget agreement, the Clean Air Act, those kind of bills. I think the Administration has been indifferent to a lot of conservative concerns."

Prince, a staunch right-wing Christian, comes from a powerful Michigan Republican family, and his father, Edgar, was a close friend of former Republican presidential candidate and antichoice leader Gary Bauer. In 1988 the elder Prince helped Bauer start the Family Research Council. Erik Prince's sister, Betsy, once chaired the Michigan Republican Party and is married to Dick DeVos, whose father, billionaire Richard DeVos, is co-founder of the major Republican benefactor Amway. Dick DeVos is also a big-time contributor to the Republican Party and will likely be the GOP candidate for Michigan governor in 2006. Another Blackwater founder, president Gary Jackson, is also a major contributor to Republican campaigns.

After the killing of four Blackwater mercenaries in Falluja in March 2004, Erik Prince hired the Alexander Strategy Group, a PR firm with close ties to GOPers like DeLay. By mid-November the company was reporting 600 percent growth. In February 2005 the company hired Ambassador Cofer Black, former coordinator for counterterrorism at the State Department and former director of the CIA's Counterterrorism Center, as vice chairman. Just as the hurricane was hitting, Blackwater's parent company, the Prince Group, named Joseph Schmitz, who had just resigned as the Pentagon's Inspector General, as the group's chief operating officer and general counsel.

While juicing up the firm's political connections, Prince has been advocating greater use of private security in international operations, arguing at a symposium at the National Defense Industrial Association earlier this year that firms like his are more efficient than the military. In May Blackwater's Jackson testified before Congress in an effort to gain lucrative Homeland Security contracts to train 2,000 new Border Patrol agents, saying Blackwater understands "the value to the government of one-stop shopping." With President Bush using the Katrina disaster to try to repeal Posse Comitatus (the ban on using U.S. troops in domestic law enforcement) and Blackwater and other security firms clearly initiating a push to install their paramilitaries on U.S. soil, the war is coming home in yet another ominous way. As one Blackwater mercenary said, "This is a trend. You're going to see a lot more guys like us in these situations."

Pat Robertson's Katrina Cash

by Max Blumenthal

[posted online on September 7, 2005]

EVERY CLOUD HAS a silver lining. Hurricane Katrina has devastated New Orleans, leaving thousands dead and hundreds of thousands homeless, and plunging the entire city into chaos. In the hurricane's wake, the Federal Emergency Management Agency (FEMA) and its director, Michael Brown, forced out of his former job at the International Arabian Horse Association, with no credentials in disaster relief, have become targets of withering criticism. Yet FEMA's relief efforts have brought considerable assistance to at least one man who stands to benefit from Hurricane Katrina perhaps more than any other individual: Pat Robertson.

With the Bush Administration's approval, Robertson's $66 million relief organization, Operation Blessing, has been prominently featured on FEMA's list of charitable groups accepting donations for hurricane relief. Dozens of media outlets, including the *New York Times*, CNN and the Associated Press, duly reprinted FEMA's list, unwittingly acting as agents soliciting cash for Robertson. "How in the heck did that happen?" Richard Walden, president of the disaster-relief group Operation USA, asked of Operation Blessing's inclusion on FEMA's list. "That gives Pat Robertson millions of extra dollars."

Operation USA has conducted disaster relief for more than twenty-five years on five continents, but like scores of other secular relief groups helping victims of Hurricane Katrina, it was omitted from FEMA's list. In fact, only two non-"faith-based" organizations were included. (One of them, the American Red Cross, is being blocked from entering New Orleans by FEMA's parent agency, the Department of Homeland Security.) FEMA, meanwhile, has reportedly turned away Wal-Mart trucks carrying food and water to the stricken city, teams of firemen from Maryland and Texas, volunteer morticians and a convoy of 1,000 boat owners offering to help rescue stranded flood victims. While relief efforts falter in the face of colossal bureaucratic incompetence, the Bush Administration's promotion of Operation Blessing has ensured that the floodwaters swallowing New Orleans will be a rising tide lifting Robertson's boat.

Robertson recently ignited a media firestorm when he called for the assassination of Venezuelan president Hugo Chávez during a broadcast of *The 700 Club*. He has also blamed the 9/11 attacks on America's tolerance of abortion and homosexuality and declared the Supreme Court a greater threat to the United States than Al Qaeda. Robertson assiduously cultivates his celebrity with remarks like these, casting himself as a divisive bigot to his foes and a righteous prophet to his allies in Christian right circles. But there is much more to Robertson than the headline-grabbing hothead he plays on TV.

Far from the media's gaze, Robertson has used the tax-exempt, nonprofit Operation Blessing as a front for his shadowy financial schemes, while exerting his influence within the GOP to cover his tracks. In 1994 he made an emotional plea on *The 700 Club* for cash donations to Operation Blessing to support airlifts of refugees from the Rwandan civil war to Zaire (now Congo). Reporter Bill Sizemore of *The Virginian Pilot* later discovered that Operation Blessing's planes were transporting diamond-mining equipment for the African Development Corporation, a Robertson-owned venture initiated with the cooperation of Zaire's then-dictator Mobutu Sese Seko.

After a lengthy investigation, Virginia's Office of Consumer Affairs determined that Robertson "willfully induced contributions from the public through the use of misleading statements and other implications." Yet when the office called for legal action against Robertson in 1999, Virginia Attorney General Mark Earley, a Republican, intervened with his own report, agreeing that Robertson had made deceptive appeals but overruling the recommendation for his prosecution. Two years earlier, while Virginia's investigation was gathering steam, Robertson donated $35,000 to Earley's campaign—Earley's largest contribution. With Earley's report came a sense of vindication. "From the very beginning," Robertson claimed, "we were trying to provide help and assistance to those who were facing disease and death in the war-torn, chaotic nation of Zaire."

(Earley is now president of Prison Fellowship Ministries, an evangelical social-work organization founded by born-again, former Nixon dirty-trickster Charles Colson. PFM has accepted

White House faith-based-initiative money and is currently engaged in hurricane relief efforts in Louisiana. Earley remains a close ally of Robertson.)

Absolved of his sins, Robertson dug his heels back in African soil. In 1999 he signed an $8 million agreement with Liberian tyrant Charles Taylor that guaranteed Robertson's Freedom Gold Ltd.—an offshore company registered to the same address as his Christian Broadcasting Network—mining rights in Liberia, and gave Taylor a 10 percent stake in the company. When the United States intervened in Liberia in 2003, forcing Taylor and the Al Qaeda operatives he was harboring to flee, Robertson accused President Bush of "undermining a Christian, Baptist president to bring in Muslim rebels to take over the country."

Robertson's scheming hasn't abated one bit. He is accused of violating his ministry's tax-exempt, nonprofit status by using it to market a diet shake he licensed this August to the health chain General Nutrition Corp. (Robertson continues to advertise the shake on his personal website.) He has withstood criticism from fellow evangelicals for investing $520,000 in a racehorse named Mr. Pat, violating biblical admonitions against gambling. He was even accused of "Jim Crow-style racial discrimination" by black employees who successfully sued his Christian Coalition in 2001 for forcing them to enter its offices through a back door and eat in a segregated area (Robertson has since resigned).

The Bush Administration has studiously overlooked Robertson's misdeeds. In October 2002, just months after he denounced the White House's faith-based initiative as "a real Pandora's box"—and one month before midterm elections—Robertson pocketed $500,000 in government grants to

Operation Blessing. Since then, with the sole exception of his criticism of the U.S. intervention in Liberia, Robertson has served as a willing surrogate for the Administration. His Regent University gave John Ashcroft a cushy professorship to cool his heels after his contentious tenure as U.S. Attorney General. And Robertson's legal foundation, the American Center for Law and Justice, is spearheading the effort to rally right-wing Christian support for Judge John G. Roberts, Jr.'s, confirmation as Chief Justice of the Supreme Court.

Now, as fallout from the President's handling of Hurricane Katrina threatens to derail the GOP's long-term agenda, Robertson is back at the plate for Bush, echoing the White House's line that state and local authorities—and even the disaster victims themselves—are to blame for the tragedy engulfing New Orleans.

The September 5 edition of *The 700 Club* included a report by Christian Broadcasting Network correspondent Gary Lane from outside the ruined New Orleans Convention Center, which had housed mostly impoverished black disaster victims throughout the weekend. "A number of possessions left behind suggest the mindset of some of the evacuees," Lane said. "They include this voodoo cup with the saying, 'May the curse be with you.' " A shot of a plastic souvenir cup from one of New Orleans's countless trinket shops appeared on the screen. "Also music CDs with the titles *Guerrilla Warfare* and *Thugs 'R' Us*," Lane stated, pointing out a pile of rap CDs strewn on the ground.

The 700 Club's featured guest was Wellington Boone, a black minister invited by Robertson to provide a counterpoint to the ubiquitous Rev. Jesse Jackson. Boone is a member of the Coalition on Revival, a Christian Reconstructionist organization that advocates replacing the U.S. Constitution with biblical law. Throughout his career, he has distinguished himself from his black clerical colleagues with such remarks as "I believe that slavery, and the understanding of it when you see it God's way, was redemptive" and "The black community must stop criticizing Uncle Tom. He is a role model."

Though Boone's appearance on *The 700 Club* consisted mostly of benign appeals for "laser-beam prayer," CBN featured a separate interview with Boone on its Web site in which he declared, "We need to consider the culture of those people still stranded in New Orleans. The looting of property, the trashing of property, et cetera, speaks to the basic character of the people." He added, "These people who have gone through slavery, segregation and the Voting Rights Act are doing this to themselves."

Boone's appearance on *The 700 Club* had been preceded by an interview with Operation Blessing President Bill Horan. Horan discussed his group's activities in Biloxi, Mississippi, where it plans to set up a mobile kitchen, and in Houston, Dallas and Beaumont, Texas, where it is disbursing cash grants to numerous, mostly unspecified mega-churches, purportedly to support their work with evacuated hurricane victims.

As for the people still stranded in New Orleans who "are doing this to themselves," as Boone said, Operation Blessing has a special plan: avoid them like the plague.

"I've actually heard reports that they [the people of Mississippi] were in worse trouble" than those in New Orleans, claimed Gordon Robertson, the son of Pat Robertson and vice president of *The 700 Club*. "They were actually harder hit."

"Oh, absolutely," agreed Horan.

At the segment's conclusion, Gordon Robertson asked

Horan, "What can people do today? If you were asking for help today, what's the number-one need?"

"It's cash. Cash is what we need more than anything," Horan pleaded. "The more cash we get, the more good we can do." And the Bush Administration, through FEMA, is doing its best to insure that Pat Robertson is getting that cash just as quickly as humanly possible.

Katrina and the Coming World Oil Crunch

by Michael T. Klare

[posted online on September 6, 2005]

MORE THAN ANY other domestic disaster, Hurricane Katrina has significant implications for America's foreign and military policies. There is, of course, the obvious connection to the war in Iraq: National Guard troops that were desperately needed to conduct rescue operations in New Orleans and southern Mississippi were instead fighting a point-less war in the Middle East, and a President whose attention should have been focused on hurricane relief was instead try-ing to put a positive spin on the Iraqi Constitution debacle. The international coverage of the human tragedy of New Orleans has also torpedoed the Administration's just-announced cam-paign to enhance America's image abroad. But far more impor-tant is the impact of Katrina on the global oil supply and the resulting increase in U.S. dependence on foreign petroleum. To appreciate the significance of this, it is first necessary to conduct a quick review of the pre- and post-Katrina oil situation, both in this country and abroad.

Before Katrina, the United States was consuming 20.4 million barrels of oil per day; some 44 percent of this was being refined into gasoline for use by motor vehicles, while another 30 percent was used to make diesel and jet fuel. Continuing a long trend toward increased dependence on foreign oil, imports accounted for 58 percent of America's total petroleum supply in 2004. And here's the kicker: Of the 5.5 million barrels of oil produced every day in the United States, 28 percent (or 1.6 million barrels) came from Louisiana and adjacent areas of the Gulf of Mexico. One cannot underestimate the importance of the Gulf area in America's overall energy equation. While oil output is dropping everywhere else in the United States, it has been increasing in the Gulf, with new wells being drilled in ever-deeper waters. "Generally speaking," the Department of Energy reported in January, "Lower-48 onshore production, particularly in Texas, has fallen in recent years, while offshore (mainly Gulf of Mexico) production is rising." The Gulf Coast also houses approximately 10 percent of the nation's refining capacity and a significant share of its natural gas production.

Meanwhile, the global oil equation has become increasingly dire. While international consumption has been rising at a torrid pace, with much of the new demand coming from China and India, the frenzied search for new fields has largely come up empty. At the same time, many older fields in Mexico, Canada, Russia, Indonesia and even the Middle East have gone into decline. These developments have led some analysts to conclude that the world has reached the moment of "peak," or maximum sustainable daily oil output; others say that we have not yet reached peak but can expect to do so soon. This is not the place to elaborate on the matter, except to say that there was widespread worry about the future availability of petroleum before Katrina struck, as demonstrated by record high prices for crude. [For background on "peak" oil, see Klare, "Crude Awakening," *The Nation*, November 8, 2004.]

And then came Katrina. In the course of a few hours, the United States lost one-fifth of its domestic petroleum output. Some of this is expected to come back on stream in the weeks ahead, but it is doubtful that all of the offshore rigs in the Gulf itself will ever be operational again. On top of this, most of the refineries in the Gulf Coast area are shut down, and imports of oil have been hampered by the damage to oil ports and unloading facilities. How quickly all of these installations can be repaired is not currently known. With no idle facilities elsewhere in the nation to replace lost Gulf capacity, supplies are likely to remain sparse (and prices high) for months to come.

But it is not the short-term picture that we should worry about the most; it is the long-term situation. This is so because the Gulf was the only area of the United States that showed any promise of compensating for the decline of older onshore fields and thus of dampening, to some degree, the nation's thirst for imported oil. There has been much discussion about the potential for drilling in the Arctic National Wildlife Refuge (ANWR) in Alaska, but energy professionals scoff at the prospects of obtaining significant amounts of crude there; instead, all of their attention has been on the deep waters of the Gulf. Spurred by the Bush Administration's energy plan, which calls for massive investment in deep-water fields, the big oil firms have poured billions of dollars into new offshore drilling facilities in the Gulf. Before Katrina, these facilities were expected to supply more than 12 percent of America's Lower 48 petroleum output by the end of 2005, and a much larger share in the years thereafter.

It is this promise of future oil that is most in question: Even if older, close-to-shore rigs can be brought back on line, there is considerable doubt about the viability of the billion-dollar deep-water rigs, most of which lie right along the path of recent hurricanes, including Ivan and Katrina. If these cannot be salvaged, there is no hope of slowing the rise in US dependence on imports, ANWR or no ANWR. This can mean one thing only: growing U.S. reliance on oil from Saudi Arabia, Iraq, Angola, Nigeria, Colombia, Venezuela and other conflict-torn producers in the developing world.

And it is this that should set the alarm bells ringing. If recent U.S. behavior is any indication, the Bush Administration will respond to this predicament by increasing the involvement of American military forces in the protection of foreign oil potentates (like the Saudi royal family) and the defense of overseas oil installations. American troops are already helping to defend the flow of petroleum in Iraq, Kuwait, Saudi Arabia, the United Arab Emirates, the Republic of Georgia, Colombia and offshore areas of West Africa, producing an enormous strain on the Pentagon's finances and capabilities. In addition, plans are being made to establish new U.S. bases in Azerbaijan and Kazakhstan, two promising producers, and in the oil-producing regions of Africa. [See Klare, "Imperial Reach," *The Nation*, April 25, 2005.] Given the need for even more foreign oil, these plans are likely to be accelerated in the months ahead. This means that the United States will become even more deeply embroiled in foreign oil wars, with an attendant increase in terrorist violence.

HURRICANE KATRINA HAS many distressing domestic consequences, and these should rightfully command our attention and compassion. But we must not lose sight of its foreign policy implications, as these are sure to spark new crises and disasters. We must not allow the White House to exploit our current energy woes to justify the further militarization of America's petroleum dependency, with all that entails. Along with other critical measures, we should use this time of reflection and reconstruction to fashion a new national energy policy, based above all on conservation and the rapid development of petroleum alternatives.

The Reconstruction
of New Oraq

By Tom Engelhardt and Nick Turse

[posted on Tomdispatch.com and Thenation.com on September 13, 2005]

"At times it is hard to ignore the comparisons between Baghdad (where I was less than a month ago and have spent more of the last two years) and New Orleans: The anarchy, the looting, some of it purely for survival, some of it purely opportunistic. We watched a flatbed truck drive by, a man on the back with an M-16 looking up on the roofs for snipers, as is common in Iraq. Private security contractors were stationed outside the Royal St. Charles Hotel; when asked if things were getting pretty wild around the area, one of them replied, 'Nope. It's pretty Green Zone here.' " (David Enders, "Surviving New Orleans," *Mother Jones* online)

IN THE DECADE before September 11th, 2001, "globalization," a word now largely missing-in-action, was on everyone's lips and we constantly heard about what a small, small world this really was. In the aftermath of Katrina, that global smallness has grown positively claustrophobic and particularly predatory. Iraq and New Orleans now seem to be morphing into a single entity, New Oraq, to be devoured by the same limited set of corporations, let loose and overseen by the same small set of Bush administration officials. In George Bush's new world of globalization, first comes the destruction and only then does one sit down at the planetary table to sup.

In recent weeks, news has been seeping out of Iraq that the "reconstruction" of that country is petering out, because the money is largely gone. According to American officials, reported T. Christian Miller of the *Los Angeles Times* last week, "The U.S. will halt construction work on some water and power plants in Iraq because it is running out of money for projects." A variety of such reconstruction projects crucial to the everyday lives of Iraqis, the British *Guardian* informs us, are now "grinding to a halt" as "plans to overhaul the country's infrastructure have been downsized, postponed or abandoned because the $24 billion budget approved by Congress has been dwarfed by the scale of the task."

Water and sanitation projects have been particularly hard hit; while staggering sums, once earmarked for reconstruction, are being shunted to private security firms whose hired-guns are assigned to guard the projects that can't be done. With funds growing scarce, various corporations closely connected to the Bush administration, having worked the Iraqi disaster for all it was worth (largely under no-bid, cost-plus contracts), are now looking New Orleans-ward.

GROUND ZERO IRAQ

THE AMERICAN OCCUPATION of Iraq began in April 2003 with a prolonged moment of chaos that set the stage for everything to follow. In the first days after Baghdad fell, the occupying army stood by idly (guarding only the Oil Ministry and the intelligence services) while Iraqi looters swept away the institutional, administrative, and cultural underpinnings of the country. The newly installed Coalition Provisional Authority (CPA), soon to be led by American viceroy L. Paul Bremer, followed up by promptly disbanding the only institution that remained half-standing, the Iraqi military. At the same time, a new American administration was set up inside the increasingly well-fortified and isolated Green Zone in Baghdad, staffed largely by Bush cronies. ("Neocon kindergarten" was the way some insiders derisively referred to the young Bush supporters sent out from Washington to staff the lower levels of the CPA for months at a time.)

The CPA then instituted a flat tax, abolished tariffs, swept away laws that might have prevented the foreign ownership of Iraqi companies, allowed the full repatriation of profits abroad, and threatened to reduce state-sponsored food and fuel subsidies. For Iraqis, this was more than just "shock and awe"; it was to be caught in the whirlwind. Call it Year Zero for Iraq or Ground Zero for the new Bush order. Iraq, stripped for action, was ready to be strip-mined—and it was then that Washington called in its crony corporations to "reconstruct" the land.

Leading the list was Kellogg, Brown & Root (KBR), a subsidiary of the energy firm Halliburton, the mega-corporation Vice President Dick Cheney once presided over. From providing fuel to building bases, doing KP to supplying laundry soap, it supported the newly privatized, stripped-down American military—and for that it "received more money from the U.S. involvement in Iraq than any other contractor," a sum that has already crested ten billion dollars with no end in sight. The Bechtel Corporation, the San Francisco-based engineering firm, known at home for its staggering cost overruns on Boston's "Big Dig" and its especially close ties to the Republican Party, raked in almost $3 billion in Iraq reconstruction contracts just in the nine months after the fall of Saddam Hussein. Fluor Corporation, an Orange County, California-based firm that inked a joint $1.1 billion deal with a London company in 2004 for "construction services for water distribution and treatment systems in Iraq" was a winner; as was the Shaw Group Inc. which, in early 2004, opened a Baghdad office to support "an approximately $47 million task order in Iraq for facility upgrades, installation of utilities and other infrastructure improvements" and was also awarded a separate $88.7 million construction deal, among other contracts. Another successful bidder in the Iraqi lottery was CH2M Hill, a Colorado-based company that, in a joint venture, took in a $28.5 million reconstruction contract in 2004 and teamed up with other contractors for a $12.7 million electrical power generation deal. These firms were joined at the table by other heavy-hitters and a dizzying array of smaller-fry American subcontractors, from the KBR-connected food service company Event Source to Bechtel's marine survey subcontractor Titan Maritime.

Over two years after the American superpower occupied Iraq and called in its reconstructors, however, the scorecard for "reconstruction" looked remarkably like one for deconstruction. The country was essentially looted and no one was left on guard, not even at the Oil Ministry. Money was spent profligately, and sometimes evidently simply pilfered. L. Paul Bremer himself reputedly had a slush fund of $600 million dollars in cash for which, according to Ed Harriman (who did a superb study of the various reports by U.S. auditors on the ensuing mayhem in the *London Review of Books*), there was "no paperwork."

When Bremer left Baghdad in June of last year, the CPA had already run through $20 billion dollars in Iraqi funds, mostly generated by oil revenues and earmarked for "the benefit of the Iraqi people" (though only $300 million in U.S. funds). Much of it seems to have gone to American companies for their various reconstruction tasks. U.S. auditors, Harriman reports, "have so far referred more than a hundred contracts, involving billions of dollars paid to American personnel and corporations, for investigation and possible criminal prosecution." It was evidently a field day of malfeasance and—a particular signature of the Bush administration—lack of accountability. In the meantime, KBR was massively overcharging the Pentagon for all those privatized tasks the military no longer cared to do, while its officials were living the good life. (Typically, KBR's "tiger team" of accountants, sent out to Kuwait to check on company overcharges, stayed in a five-star hotel to the tune of $1 million in taxpayer money.)

The results we now know well. Electricity and oil production, for instance, still remain at or below the figures for the worst days of Saddam Hussein's embattled regime; and on that cleared land at Ground Zero Iraq, a fierce resistance movement rages, while, from Basra to Mosul, disappointment with and disapproval of the American occupiers only grows.

Now, these same corporations are being loosed on the South-eastern United States on the same no-bid, cost-plus basis. Like Baghdad and much of Iraq, New Orleans and the Mississippi coast have just experienced "shock and awe"—Katrina's winds and waters, not U.S. cruise missiles. With troops occupying New Orleans, the Bush administration–allied corporations of the whirlwind that feed off chaos and destruction are already moving in. In this sense, the next wave of chaos has, from their point of view, arrived like the proverbial cavalry, just in the nick of time.

BRINGING THE POST-WAR HOME

As REUTERS REPORTED recently, "A slowing of reconstruction work in Iraq has freed up people for Fluor Corp. to begin rebuilding in the U.S. Gulf Coast region after Hurricane Katrina, the big engineering and construction company's chairman and chief executive said on Friday. 'Our rebuilding work in Iraq is slowing down and this has made some people available to respond to our work in Louisiana,' Fluor chief Alan Boeckmann said in a telephone interview." And Fluor responded in a thoroughly reasonable way—they put an experienced man on the job, sending their "senior project manager" in Iraq to Louisiana.

In fact, with Congress already making a $62 billion initial down payment on post-Katrina reconstruction work, the Bush administration has just given out its first 6 reconstruction contracts, five of them—could anyone be surprised—to Iraqi reconstructors, including Fluor. Small world indeed. The Bush version of crony capitalism should perhaps be termed predatory capitalism, following as it does so closely in the wake of war and natural disaster much as camp followers used to trail armies, ready, in case of victory, to loot the baggage train of the enemy.

But let's pull back for a moment and try to reconstruct, however briefly, at least a modest picture of the massively interconnected world of the reconstructors. A good place to start is with George Bush's pal Joseph Allbaugh, a member of his "so-called iron triangle of trusted Texas cohorts." Allbaugh seems to display in his recent biography just about every linkage that makes New Oraq what it is clearly becoming. He ran the Bush presidential campaign of 2000; and subsequently was installed as the director of FEMA which, in congressional testimony, he characterized as "an overstuffed entitlement program," counseling (as Harold Meyerson of the *American Prospect* pointed out recently) "states and cities to rely instead on 'faith-based organizations . . . like the Salvation Army and the Mennonite Disaster Service.'"

As at the Coalition Provisional Authority in Baghdad, so at FEMA in Washington, the larder of administrators would soon be stocked with second and third-rate Bush supporters and cronies. Five of FEMA's top eight managers would, according to Spencer S. Hsu of the *Washington Post*, arrive with "virtually no experience in handling disasters," three of them "with ties to President Bush's 2000 campaign or to the White House advance operation." A "brain drain" of competent administrators followed as—à la the Pentagon—FEMA's focus turned to the war on terror, money was drained from natural-disaster work, and the agency was "privatized" with crucial activities outsourced to Bush-friendly corporations.

In March 2003, Allbaugh departed FEMA, putting the increasingly starved and down-sized operation in the hands of

Michael Brown, an old college buddy whose previous job had been overseeing the International Arabian Horse Association. He then made his faith-based career choice—no, not to join the Salvation Army or the Mennonite Disaster Service. Instead he opted for what the Bush administration really believed in—both in Iraq and at home. He became a high-priced consultant/lobbyist, founding in the ensuing years three consulting firms. At Blackwell Fairbanks, LLC, he teamed up with Andrew Lundquist, who led the Dick Cheney task force that produced the administration's National Energy Policy, to "successfully represen[t] clients before the executive and legislative branches of the United States government." Then there was the Allbaugh Company through which he represents Halliburton's KBR as well as military-industrial powerhouse Northrop Grumman. Finally, there was New Bridge Strategies, LLC, where he serves as chairman and director. New Bridge Strategies bills itself as "a unique company that was created specifically with the aim of assisting clients to evaluate and take advantage of business opportunities in the Middle East following the conclusion of the U.S.-led war in Iraq."

Not surprisingly, the firm's vice chairman and director, Ed Rogers (who, during the "2004 campaign cycle . . . made over 150 live TV news appearances defending and promoting the Bush administration") also serves as vice chairman of the consulting firm Barbour, Griffith & Rogers, Inc. (which he founded with Haley Barbour, now the governor of storm-battered Mississippi); New Bridge's Director, Lanny Griffith, who serves as the CEO of Barbour, Griffith & Rogers, "was national chairman for the Bush/Cheney Entertainment Task Force and coordinated entertainment for the 2001 Bush Inaugural." He was, typically enough, one of the 2004 Bush campaign's "Rangers"—an elite group of fundraisers, each of whom was responsible for gathering up over $200,000 for the President; while New Bridge Strategies' Advisory Board Member Jamal Daniel is "a Principal with Crest Investment Company"—a firm co-chaired by the president's younger brother Neil.

In answer to critics who claimed he and others were cashing in on their service to Bush and Cheney, Allbaugh responded, "I don't buy the 'revolving door' argument. This is America. We all have a right to make a living."

As President and CEO at Allbaugh Co. and assumedly as a former head of FEMA, not to say as close friend and mentor to FEMA's (now departed) head and as a Presidential pal, he found himself at the front of the Katrina disaster line, apparently pushing hard (although he denied it) for such companies as— you guessed it—KBR and the Shaw Group. By September 7 at the latest, unlike the administration, he was down in Louisiana surveying the damage in the Gulf Coast and the wreckage of the agency he once presided over, while directing his clients to the lucrative world of American disaster, now that the lucrative world of Iraqi disaster had been sucked reasonably dry.

GROUND ZERO NEW ORLEANS

ON SEPTEMBER 12, 2005, the *Wall Street Journal* reported, "FEMA and the Army Corps of Engineers have awarded six contracts, most for as much as $100 million, for recovery and rebuilding work." It should be of little surprise that the Shaw Group landed two of these $100 million deals (a FEMA contract to refurbish existing buildings and for other emergency housing tasks as well as an Army Corps of Engineers contract to aid recovery efforts, including pumping water from New Orleans). Others on the list included a who's who of favorite Bush administration contractors from Iraq: Bechtel, Fluor, and CH2M Hill (all signed on to construct temporary housing). In fact, of the companies on the *Journal*'s list, only one (Dewberry, LLC) was not, apparently, involved in Iraq. Halliburton was, of course, not left out in the cold. In the immediate aftermath of the hurricane, its KBR subsidiary reaped "$29.8 million in Pentagon contracts to begin rebuilding Navy bases in Louisiana and Mississippi."

These companies, however, aren't the only ones returning from Iraq, like so many predator drones, to pick up lucrative deals. In the wake of Katrina, Intelsat, a global satellite services provider that, in Iraq, had teamed up with Bechtel on a big USAID reconstruction program, agreed to new post-Katrina contracts with the Defense Department and FEMA. Similarly, just two days after Katrina ravaged the Gulf Coast, the Air National Guard contracted with another satellite services provider, Segovia, which, according to a 2004 company press release, had "emerged as a key telecommunications provider for the Iraqi reconstruction efforts."

Along with their service in Iraq, the Katrina reconstruction companies are tied together in another important way. They tend to be particularly well linked to the Bush administration and the Republican Party. As former Oklahoma Republican Governor Frank Keating said of Allbaugh, "Joe . . . knows how elected officials and appointed officials like me think and work, and that culture is a fraternity." Halliburton, for instance, picked off "another high-level Bush appointee, Kirk Van Tine, earlier this year to work as a lobbyist. Similarly, in 2001, Bush appointed Robert G. Card, then a senior vice president at CH2M Hill, undersecretary at the U.S. Department of Energy, a position he held until 2004. Today, Card is the president and group chief executive of the International Group at CH2M Hill.

Not surprisingly, during the 2004 election season, CH2M Hill was the top "construction services" contributor to political campaigns, sending nearly 70 percent of its $476,800 in contributions to Republican candidates. In fact, fourteen people on the CH2M payroll contributed to Bush's 2004 campaign, including the company's chairman and CEO, president, senior vice-president, and president of regional operations, each of whom gave between $1,000 and $2,000. Meanwhile, Bechtel's political action committee contributed 68 percent of its funds to Republican candidates and causes; while Halliburton, which ranks among the top twenty "Oil and Gas" contributors to political campaigns, handed out 87 percent of its money to Republicans.

Theoretically, there should be nothing more glorious than the job of healing the war-torn or rebuilding the lives of those devastated by natural disaster, nor anything more relevant to government. Unfortunately, in the case of KBR World, there's nothing glorious about it, except the 5-star hotels for the reconstructors. Prediction is usually a dismal science for any writer. In this case, however, it's already easy to imagine—as some Democrats in Congress are beginning to do—the consequences of Bush-style "reconstruction" in the United States.

Those no-bid, cost-plus contracts already being dealt out to the usual suspects tell you what you need to know about future cost-overruns, klepto-reconstruction activities, and the like which are practically guaranteed to deconstruct the bulk of the Gulf Coast and leave New Orleans, the destroyed parts of Mississippi, and the hundreds of thousands of evacuees, not to speak of Congress, gasping for breath amid a landscape largely sucked dry, not of water, but of cash and sustenance.

George Bush's version of capitalism is of a predatory, parasitical kind. It feeds on death, eats money, goes home when the cash stops flowing, and leaves further devastation in its wake. New Orleans, like a rotting corpse, naturally attracts all sorts of flies. Reports have been trickling in that the private security firms—call them mercenary corporations like Blackwater USA—which have flooded Iraq with an estimated twenty to twenty-five thousand hired guns (some paid up to $1,000 a day), have been taking the same route back to New Orleans and the Mississippi coast as KBR, Bechtel, and the Shaw Group.

THEY FIRST ARRIVED in the employ of private corporations and local millionaires who wanted their property protected. A week or so into September, however, Jeremy Scahill and Daniela Crespo of Democracy Now! found the hired-guns of Blackwater cruising the streets of New Orleans, carrying assault weapons, claiming to have been deputized, insisting that they were working for the Homeland Security Department and that they were sleeping in camps the Department had organized. ("When they told me New Orleans, I said, 'What country is that in?,'" said one of the Blackwater men.) Then, on September 13, the *Washington Post* reported that "Blackwater USA, known for its work supporting military operations in Iraq, said it would provide 164 armed guards to help provide security at FEMA sites in Louisiana."

Today, New Orleans' streets are under military occupation; its property is guarded by hired guns; and the corporations of the whirlwind are pouring into town. All that's missing is the insurgency.

Left to Die

by Billy Sothern

[from the January 2, 2006 issue]

I F, AS DOSTOYEVSKY claimed, the degree of civiliza-
tion of a society can be measured by the treatment of
its prisoners, we are in even deeper trouble in New Orleans than
many realize. In this city, under the radar of most media, the
biggest prison crisis since Attica is unfolding. And no one
seems to care, because despite Hurricane Katrina's having
"exposed" American poverty and racism, mass incarceration of
poor black Americans remains an accepted, if overlooked, fact
of modern life. After all, the thinking goes, they did the crime,
now they have to do the time. However, like everything else in
New Orleans, it's not so simple.

The New Orleans jail complex sits behind the old gothic
Orleans Parish Criminal Court and backs up to Interstate 10
in a run-down area of the city. On the days following Katrina,
the entire complex sat beneath many feet of water. At that time

the jails housed more than 8,000 prisoners, the majority of whom were pretrial detainees, people with the fundamental presumption of innocence but without the funds for bail or a lawyer to get them out before trial. There was a larger than usual population of pretrial inmates when the storm came because before it arrived the police had conducted sweeps to clear the streets, picking up people for petty crimes like loitering or trespassing, and because other parish jails had evacuated their prisoners to New Orleans.

Despite the universal awareness of the risk of flooding in the city, the low-lying jail failed to execute any real evacuation plan. Instead, even faster than New Orleans police abandoned the citizens of New Orleans, many of the sheriff's deputies who guard the city's prisoners abandoned their charges and left men and women wondering whether they were going to die as water rose in their locked cells. As prisoner Dan Bright told Human Rights Watch, "They left us to die there."

Prisoners helped one another escape the flood by prying open cell doors, breaking through windows and finding higher ground in the jail. While officials deny that any bodies were found, many prisoners who were there insist that they saw floating bodies. Those who made it out were rounded up by the few remaining guards and gathered on a nearby interstate overpass. People remained there for almost two days—without water, under the sun—appearing as a blur of orange jumpsuits from the CNN cameras in helicopters flying above. They were left to urinate and defecate on themselves, hampered by restraints so tight that a month later attorneys who visited them could still see dark purple bands around their wrists. Eventually buses arrived and the detainees were transferred randomly to prisons around the state, but without the papers that might easily distinguish a person who had been arrested for illegally reading tarot cards or "angling without a license" from someone charged with a serious, violent crime.

As bad as this was, it was only the beginning of the indignities the evacuated prisoners were to face. They found themselves in an impromptu patchwork of overcrowded state prisons, parish jails and facilities opened just to accommodate evacuated prisoners. The unluckiest among them, mostly from Jefferson Parish, found themselves at Jena Correctional, a former juvenile prison owned by the Wackenhut Corrections Corporation that was closed after the Juvenile Justice Project of Louisiana, Human Rights Watch and the Justice Department exposed widespread beatings of incarcerated children there in the late 1990s. That spirit was kept alive in the new incarnation of the prison: Evacuated prisoners were routinely and viciously beaten by their jailers, guards from other facilities who were without a chain of command and for whom there was zero possibility of accountability. Rachel Jones of the Louisiana Capital Assistance Center, a pro bono attorney who was working there at the time, told me that after being a public defender in Brooklyn and a capital trial attorney in Louisiana, "I have never seen anything like it."

JONES SAID THE inmates were bruised all over their bodies. They passed her little notes saying "help" when the guards weren't looking and reported that guards were calling them "nigger" and "boy." When she returned days later to follow up, they had been brutalized even more; some reported having received beatings from guards as retaliation. After visiting with many inmates at various prisons and jails, it became clear to her that these incidents were widespread, and she made it her top priority to get guys who didn't belong there out of jail.

Jones and a handful of other lawyers, including Phyllis Mann, a veteran Louisiana criminal defense attorney, began poring over the available records on the evacuated inmates and found thousands who had been unconstitutionally and illegally imprisoned. Many should have been released weeks or months earlier, as their sentences had long since expired. Some had been picked up on charges in the days before the storm for municipal offenses like unpaid traffic tickets and had never been before a judge, as required by the Constitution. Others were simply sitting in jail, awaiting trial for minor crimes for which the maximum sentence was far less than the amount of time they had already served. While some of these people have been released in the past month, many remain incarcerated and separated from their families when they are most needed. For example, as recently as mid-November, David Moffett, a 43-year-old man from New Orleans, was still incarcerated in a Bossier Parish jail on a ten-day sentence begun August 22 for public drunkenness.

Who was there to make sure that these citizens, victims of one of the country's worst natural disasters, were not further deprived of their Eighth Amendment right to dignified treatment as prisoners, their right to due process under law and their right to the presumption of innocence? There was no public defender's office zealously fighting for their rights because New Orleans has no real public defender's office. Nor was there a crusading prisoners' rights organization on the ground to provide meaningful oversight of the state's treatment of its vulnerable wards. Beyond the handful of volunteer lawyers, no one was there for these people, and though the volunteers have been diligent, their work has not been sufficient to address the needs of everyone.

It is hard to believe that a state with one of the highest per capita incarceration rates in the United States—which itself is a world leader in incarceration—does not have a single organization or agency dedicated to the rights of prisoners, but it's true. Sadly, by orders of magnitude, there were more rescue people in Louisiana to protect the "animal rights" of dogs than there were lawyers or activists to protect the human rights of thousands of our citizens.

While New Orleans does not have a full-time public defender, the city is obligated by the Sixth Amendment of the Constitution, like every other town in the United States, to provide free attorneys to poor people who are otherwise unable to defend themselves against charges leveled by the state. That service in New Orleans is provided through the Orleans Parish Indigent Defender Board, which contracts with a group of part-time attorneys who, when they are not taking paid cases or writing wills and estates for their regular clients, are assigned to represent the thousands of poor people annually charged with crimes in New Orleans. Like so many things in the city, these part-time contracts have become patronage positions appointed more on the basis of fealty to political players than concern for the rights of the accused. In the weeks and months after the storm, these public defenders were nowhere to be found, although they were counsel of record for nearly all the evacuated prisoners. When asked about the prison crisis and his concerns about the rights of his clients, Tilden Greenbaum, head of the Indigent Defender Board, told the New York Times his clients were being patient. "Sooner or later, we're going to have to start making noise about it," he said. "But given the magnitude of what everybody's been through, now is not the time to push."

Meg Garvey, another pro bono lawyer who has been working with evacuated inmates, isn't feeling patient at all. She started pushing months ago to try to help these clients. "So many of these guys were in here for minor stuff, and when the storm came their communication with their families was completely cut off," she said. "They couldn't be part of keeping their families safe or together. Now the world is changing dramatically while they are in prison. Babies are born. Their grandma dies. Their family resettles in Texas. And they are in for nothing. They are desperate to return to their families."

Given all the minor things with which people ordinarily run out of patience, like rush-hour traffic and long lines at the bank, it is hard to imagine much patience from people who have been unconstitutionally detained for months after a nightmarish experience of rising water in a locked cell. Certainly, it is inappropriate for their lawyers to be counseling patience while they are wrongfully imprisoned. However, according to Garvey, the prisoners are incredibly patient, and they're grateful for the assistance from the handful of lawyers who offered help without any expectation of compensation and disregarding the turmoil that their own lives had been thrown into by the storm. For the rest of us, that there are a few pro bono lawyers providing a constitutionally mandated service the government is neglecting and has neglected for decades should sting, not give comfort.

New Orleans needs a politically independent public defender's office—one that not only provides the minimum representation guaranteed by the Constitution but that deals holistically with clients, their families and their communities. Such an agency could begin to address the collateral consequences that mass incarceration has on the families and communities where a large percentage of adult men are behind bars. Further, we need public institutions dedicated to the principle that the rights of prisoners are not mere abstractions but guarantees, and that there are actual remedies when those rights are violated. This is imperative in a state where incarceration has become the one-size-fits-all response to social ills caused by failed schools, a decimated economy and meager and crumbling public housing.

Here as elsewhere, such institutions do not need heaps of money. They require instead a change of attitude—whereby people deprived of their personal liberty are still valued and protected by society. In the legal defense context, this means dedicated, full-time public defenders insulated from political pressure, like the Public Defender Service in Washington, D.C., or the Bronx Defenders in New York City—offices of true believers who make the adversarial process a challenge to the state's immense power to incarcerate and even kill its citizens.

The storm created opportunities for structural reform in areas where the government has long failed its citizens. With the city's dysfunctional indigent defense almost nonexistent, this may be the only chance in a generation to re-create a major urban public defense system in a manner that addresses the impact of criminalization and mass incarceration on poor families while providing constitutionally mandated services.

New Orleans is a struggling city in one of the poorest parts of the country. We have been flattened by a storm. There are of course many other pressing needs as we rebuild the city and the region. But if we are ever going to be a civilized city, or country, we are going to have to begin to work as hard for the weakest and most maligned among us as we do for the strongest and most sympathetic. If we don't, any of us could one day face the consequences.

PART

THREE

A People's Reconstruction

Hurricane Gumbo

by Mike Davis and Anthony Fontenot

[from the November 7, 2005 issue]

EVANGELINE PARISH, LOUISIANA

NOTHING IS MOVING in Evangeline Parish except for the sky. Black rain bands, the precursors of Hurricane Rita's fury, scud by at disconcerting velocity. Wind gusts uproot ancient oaks and topple a decrepit billboard advertising an extinct brand of chewing tobacco. The rice fields are flooding and the roads are barricaded with tree debris.

Millions of desperate Texans and southern Louisianans are still gridlocked on interstate highways headed north from Rita's path, but here in Ville Platte, a town of 11,000 in the heart of Acadiana (French-speaking southern Louisiana), the traditional response to an impending hurricane is not to evacuate but to gather together and cook.

Dolores Fontenot, matriarch of a clan that ordinarily mobilizes forty members for Sunday dinner (the "immediate family") and

800 for a wedding (the "extended family"), is supervising the preparation of a colossal crab gumbo. Its rich aroma is sensory reassurance against the increasingly sinister machine-gunning of the rain on her home's boarded-up windows.

Although every major utility from Baton Rouge to Galveston has crashed, a noisy generator in the carport keeps lights flickering inside as little kids chase one another and older men converse worriedly about the fate of their boats and hunting camps. There are disturbing reports about the waters rising around Pecan Island, Holly Beach and Abbeville.

IN ADDITION TO Fontenot kin, the table is also set for three eminent immunologists from Latin America, whose laboratories at the Tulane and LSU medical centers in New Orleans were flooded by Katrina, destroying several years of invaluable cancer research. The doctors, two from Medellín, Colombia, and one from Mexico City, joke that Ville Platte has become the "Cajun Ark."

It is a surprisingly apt analogy. The folks of Ville Platte, a poor Cajun and black Creole community with a median income less than half that of the rest of the nation, have opened their doors over the past three weeks to more than 5,000 of the displaced people they call "company" (the words "refugee" and "evacuee" are considered too impersonal, even impolite). Local fishermen and hunters, moreover, were among the first volunteers to take boats into New Orleans to rescue desperate residents from their flooded homes.

Ville Platte's homemade rescue and relief effort—organized around the popular slogan "If not us, then who?"—stands in striking contrast to the incompetence of higher levels of government as well as to the hostility of other, wealthier towns, including some white suburbs of New Orleans, toward influxes of evacuees, especially poor people of color. Indeed, Evangeline Parish as a whole has become a surprising island of interracial solidarity and self-organization in a state better known for incorrigible racism and corruption.

What makes Ville Platte and some of its neighboring communities so exceptional?

Part of the answer, we discovered, has been the subtle growth of a regional "nationalism" that has drawn southern Louisiana's root cultures—African-American, black Creole, Cajun and French Indian—closer together in response to the grim and ever-growing threats of environmental and cultural extinction. There is a shared, painful recognition that the land is rapidly sinking and dying, as much from the onslaught of corporate globalization as from climate wrath.

If one wanted to be fashionably academic, Ville Platte's big-heartedness might be construed as a conscious response to the "postcolonial" crisis of Acadiana. In plainer language, it is an act of love in a time of danger: a radical but traditionalist gesture that defies most of the simplistic antinomies—liberal versus conservative, red state versus blue state, freedom of choice versus family values, and so on—that the media use to categorize contemporary American life.

But before arguing theory, it is first necessary to introduce some of the ordinary heroes sitting around Dolores Fontenot's generous dinner table as Rita shakes the earth outside.

THE CAJUN NAVY

EDNA FONTENOT PASSES around bottles of beer—Corona in honor of the Latin American guests. He is a lean, gentle-spirited man in his late 40s with an impressive résumé of mechanical skills and survival expertise.

"You know, we were all watching New Orleans on television and we realized that somebody's got to help all these people, because nothing was happening. Nothing. Then there was a call [by the Louisiana Department of Wildlife and Fisheries] for small boats. So I said, I'm going. I knew I could do something. I lived in New Orleans and know how to get around on water."

Edna drove to nearby Lafayette (Acadiana's informal capital city) then convoyed with scores of other boat owners to Old Metairie, across from the broken 17th Street Canal that had emptied the waters of Lake Pontchartrain into central New Orleans.

"There was no FEMA, just a big ol' bunch of Cajun guys in their boats. We tried to coordinate best we could, but it was still chaos. It was steaming hot and there was a smell of death. The people on the rooftops and overpasses were desperate. They had been there for several days in the sun with no food, no water. They were dehydrated, blistered and sick . . . giving up, you know, ready to die."

Edna stayed for two days until floating debris broke his propeller. Although FEMA has recently taken credit for the majority of rescues, Edna scoffs at its claims. Apart from the Coast Guard, he saw only the Wildlife and Fisheries' "Cajun Navy" in action. "That was it. Just us volunteers." He feels guilty that he couldn't afford to fix his boat and return. "I had some good times in that damn city," he says softly, "and, you know, I have more black friends there than white."

CITY OF THE DEAD

WHILE EDNA WAS saving the living, his brother-in-law, a police detective from another city, was engaged in the grueling, macabre work of retrieving bodies. "Vincent" (his real name can't be used) went out each night in a Fisheries boat with a scuba diver and an M-16-toting National Guard escort.

"I wore a [hazmat] space suit and piloted the boat. I was chosen because I'm trained in forensics, and since I am a Cajun the higher powers assumed I was a water baby. We worked at night because of the heat and to avoid the goddamn news helicopters that hover like vultures during the daytime. We didn't want some poor son of a bitch seeing his grandma covered with ants or crabs on the 6 o'clock news."

Ants and crabs? "Hey, this is Louisiana. The minute New Orleans flooded it became swamp again. The ecosystem returns. Ants float and they build big colonies on floating bodies the same as they would upon a cypress log. And the crabs eat carrion. We'd pulled the crabs off, but the goddamn ants were a real problem."

Vincent described the exhausting, gruesome work of hauling bloated bodies aboard the boat and then zipping them into body bags. (FEMA neglected water, food rations and medicine, but did fly thousands of body bags into Louis Armstrong Airport.) Although Vincent was supposed to tag the bags, few victims had any identification. Some didn't have faces.

• • •

ONE OF US asks about the demographics of death. "We pulled seventy-seven bodies out of the water. Half were little kids. It was tough—no one died with their eyes closed, and all had fought like hell, some slowly drowning in their attics.

"I deal with crime scenes and human remains all the time and usually keep a professional distance. You have to, if you want to continue to do your job. But sometimes a case really gets to you. We found the corpse of a woman clutching a young baby. Mother or sister, I don't know. I couldn't pry the infant out of the woman's grasp without breaking her fingers. After finally separating them, the baby left a perfect outline imprinted across the lady's chest. That will really haunt me. And so will the goddamn cries of the people we left behind.

"We were under strict orders to remove only bodies. But there were still lots of people on the roofs or leaning out the windows of their houses. They were crazy with fear and thirst. They screamed, begged and cursed us. But we had a boatload of bodies, some probably infectious. So we saved the dead and left the living." Vincent believes that the "sniper activity" so luridly reported in the media was from stranded people who were outraged when boats and helicopters ignored them.

MADONNA AND CHILD

DANNY GUIDRY, A paramedic married to a Fontenot cousin, has a story with a happier ending. Along with his partner and driver, he was sent with dozens of ambulances and rescue units from the Cajun parishes to the edge of New Orleans.

As victims were brought in by volunteers in boats or by the Coast Guard in their big Black Hawk helicopters, Danny classified them according to the severity of their condition and took the most critical cases to Baton Rouge, one and a half hours away through the pandemonium of emergency traffic.

Since southern Louisiana's only full-fledged trauma center was in a rapidly flooding hospital in New Orleans, most of the injured or sick evacuees were dropped at a triage center in a Baton Rouge sports stadium where a single nurse, just 24 years old, was in charge of sorting out cases and sending the most serious to already overwhelmed local hospitals.

"By my third trip," Danny explained, "I was working on automatic pilot. You just shut yourself off from the pain and turmoil around you and concentrate on doing your job as carefully and quickly as possible."

But, like Vincent, he found one case extraordinary. "She was a young lady, thirty-three weeks pregnant, in premature labor. She had been in a hospital ready for a caesarean section when the evacuation of the city was announced. Her physician stopped the labor and sent her home, presuming, I guess, that she had access to a car, which she didn't. Her husband went out to look for food, then the levee broke. When we picked her up, the husband had been missing for several days. To make matters more complicated, she was cradling a 9-month-old baby that she had rescued from a crack-addict neighbor. Both she and the infant were heat stressed, and my sixth sense told me she might not make it to Baton Rouge.

"It was the longest run of my career. Her IV was bad and I was running out of fluid. She was getting paler, and her blood pressure was falling dangerously. My orders were to take her to the central triage center, but I told my partner to punch it and head straight to the nearest hospital.

"Out of professional protocol I never divulge personal information to a victim. But this case really moved me, so I gave this young woman my phone number and urged her, Please call when you are out of labor. In fact, I kept phoning the hospital to monitor her progress. She had a healthy baby and eventually found her husband. Meanwhile, the infant she had saved was reunited with its mother. Having come this far with this girl, I just couldn't walk away, so my wife and I invited her and her husband to Ville Platte. We found them a little house and she's getting ready to go to college in Lafayette. I helped board up their windows this afternoon."

"JUST FRIENDS"

In between Rita's windy tantrums, we made a quick run down to the Civic Center Shelter, where volunteers welcomed new "company" from the hurricane-threatened Louisiana-Texas border area.

The shelter is supported only by local resources but provides ample beds, toys, television, Internet access, superb Cajun-Creole cooking and hospitality to evacuees staying only for a few nights or waiting to be rehoused on a medium-term basis with local residents.

The center's founders include Edna's "Kosher Cajun" cousin Mark Krasnoff (his dad was from Brooklyn) and Jennifer Vidrine, who has become its full-time coordinator. Everyone had told us that Jennifer has the most gorgeous smile in

Louisiana. Although she hadn't slept in two days, her smile indeed brightened the entire shelter.

An LSU graduate with a recent fellowship at Harvard's prestigious Kennedy School, Jennifer has had every opportunity to conquer the world, but she wouldn't think of leaving Ville Platte. She talks about the first week after Katrina.

"There were just thousands of tired, scared people on the roads of Evangeline Parish. Not just in cars: Some were walking, carrying everything they still owned in a backpack. Some were crying; they had a look of hopelessness. It was like *The Grapes of Wrath*. Most knew nothing about Ville Platte, but were amazed when we invited them into our homes."

It sounds too good to be true: Acadiana, despite deep cross-racial kinships of culture, religion and blood, was once a bastion of Jim Crow. Just a few years ago an effort by Ville Platte authorities to redistrict the town to dilute the black vote was struck down as a violation of the Voting Rights Act. So we ask Jennifer, who's both "French" and African-American, if the relief effort isn't discreetly color-coded, with a preference for suburban white refugees.

She's unflappable. "No, not at all. We embrace everyone with the same love. And the whole community supports this project: black, white, Catholic, Baptist. Perhaps one-third of all private homes have taken in out-of-town folks. And it doesn't matter where our 'company' comes from: the Ninth Ward {black} or Chalmette {white}. That's just the way we are. We're all raised to take care of neighbors and give kindness to strangers. This is what makes this little town special and why I love it so much."

Jennifer praises local schoolteachers and the City Council. But when we ask about the contribution of the national relief organizations and the federal government, she points to the banner over the shelter's entrance: NO RED CROSS, NO SALVATION ARMY OR FEDERAL FUNDS . . . JUST FRIENDS.

"I started trying to contact the Red Cross immediately. I phoned them for thirteen days straight. I was told 'no personnel are available.' [According to the *Wall Street Journal*, the Red Cross, which raised $1 billion in the name of aiding Katrina victims, had 163,000 volunteers available.] Finally, they promised to come, but then canceled at the last minute. FEMA is just the same. We have yet to see the federal government in person." Indeed, before Rita closed the roads, we saw no evidence of a federal presence, although we ran across several SUVs with Halliburton logos.

Ville Platte, whose black majority has an annual per capita income of only $5,300, has thus managed to help thousands of strangers without a single cent of Red Cross or federal aid. We remain incredulous: What superior organizational principle or charismatic leadership is responsible for such an achievement?

Jennifer is bemused. "Listen, my committee is my telephone. I call folks and they respond. Food, clothing, cots, medicine—it's all provided. Even poor people down here have some extra deer meat in the freezer or an old quilt or an extra bed. And all of us know how to spontaneously cooperate. My God, we're always organizing christenings or family gatherings. So why do we need a lot of formal leadership?" In a nation currently without competent leadership, this may be a reasonable, even deeply profound, question.

THE PEOPLE'S REPUBLIC OF THE BAYOUS?

So what does it all mean?

Mark Krasnoff thinks Ville Platte is the shape of things to come: southern Louisiana getting its interracial act together to take on its colonizers and rulers. A small, wiry man with the build of a dancer or gymnast, he is an actor (most recently in a prophetic FX network TV drama, *Oil Storm*, about a category 6 hurricane hitting the Gulf Coast) and a stunning bilingual raconteur. He is also the Che Guevara-cum-Huey Long of Evangeline Parish. His beat-up pickup wears the bumper sticker LOUISIANA: THIRD WORLD AND PROUD OF IT.

"Look, Louisiana is the same as any exploited oil-rich country—like a Nigeria or Venezuela. For generations the big oil and gas companies have pumped billions out of our bayous and offshore waters, and all we get back is coastal erosion, pollution, cancer and poverty. And now bloated bodies and dead towns.

"People in the rest of America need to understand there are no 'natural' disasters in Louisiana. This is one of the richest lands in the world—everything from sugar and crawfish to oil and sulfur—but we're neck-to-neck with Mississippi as the poorest state. Sure, Washington builds impressive levees to safeguard river commerce and the shipping industry, but do you honestly think they give a shit about blacks, Indians and coonasses [pejorative for Cajuns]? Poor people's levees, if they even existed, were about as good as our schools [among the worst in the nation]. Katrina just followed the outlines of inequality."

Mark is incandescent. "The very soul of Louisiana is now at stake." He enumerates the working-class cultures threatened with extinction: the "second line" black neighborhoods of New

Orleans, the French Indians in Houma, the Isleno (Canary Islander) and Vietnamese fishermen in Plaquemines, Cajun communities all along the Gulf Coast.

"If our 'leaders' have their way this whole goddamn region will become either a toxic graveyard or a big museum where jazz, zydeco and Cajun music will still be played for tourists but the cultures that gave them life are defunct or dispersed."

Mark's worst fears, of course, are rapidly becoming facts on the ground. Bush's Housing Secretary, Alphonso Jackson, told the *Houston Chronicle* on September 30, "I think it would be a mistake to rebuild the Ninth Ward." He predicted that New Orleans' black population, 67 percent before Katrina, would shrink to 35 to 40 percent. "New Orleans is not going to be as black as it was for a long time, if ever again," he said.

This was undoubtedly music to the ears of Republican master strategist Karl Rove, who knows that the loss of 10,000 or 15,000 active black Democratic voters could alter the balance of power in Louisiana and transform overnight a pink state into a red state. The GOP could gain another senator as well as the governorship.

Mark's preferred solution is secession: "Let us keep our oil and gas revenues and we can preserve our way of life as well. We don't really belong to the same cultural system anyway. You prize money, competition and individual success; we value family, community and celebration. Give us independence and we'll restore the wetlands, rebuild the Ninth Ward and move the capital to Evangeline Parish. If you wish, you can ship the Statue of Liberty to Ville Platte and we'll add a new inscription: Send us your tired and huddled masses and we'll feed them hurricane gumbo."

We all laugh, but everyone understands it is gallows humor. Ordinary people across Louisiana and the Gulf Coast are beginning to understand what it's like to be Palestinians or Iraqis at the receiving end of Washington's hypocritical promises and disastrous governmental and military actions.

Katrina and Rita have stripped Louisiana naked: Exposed to a brutal light are government neglect, corporate rapine and blatant ethnic cleansing. Equally revealed, however, is the bayou country's ancient moral bedrock of populist revolt, cultural resistance and New Testament generosity. But when in the entire bloody course of history has the kindness of strangers ever defeated the conspiracy of money and power?

Beyond Shelters

by Michael Tisserand

[from the November 7, 2005 issue]

A CHAIN-LINK FENCE circles the unnamed evacuee community that the Federal Emergency Management Agency has founded on the outskirts of Baker, Louisiana. Inside, hundreds of trailers have been assigned their own section letters and numbers, which are hand-scrawled on each trailer's front window. As dusk settles over Baker, residents wander down identical gravel paths, searching for new addresses.

Tanya Harris steers her dusty Camry through the gate. She slows down; nobody stops her. Harris parks near a large, unlit building that she decides must be a community hall. It's one of the few structures here that's not on wheels. Gladys Bernard, who's riding in the passenger seat, peers at the hall. "The sign says welcome," she says hopefully.

Harris, who works with Bernard at ACORN, a national community group for low- and moderate-income families, grabs an instant camera and stacks of fliers. One stack is for residents who want ACORN to field complaints about jobs, housing and other post-evacuation concerns. Other fliers announce an upcoming protest for residents of New Orleans' Lower Ninth Ward, the devastated working-class neighborhood that for weeks has remained almost entirely off-limits to residents and business owners. Harris's family has resided in the Lower Ninth Ward ever since the late 1940s, when her grandfather, a longshoreman, bought four plots of land for $200 apiece.

As Harris leads the way into the dark hall, where a few families are finishing dinner, she uncannily locates Lower Ninth neighbors. She trades addresses with one woman; they share names of people they both know. "I just want to go home, baby," the woman says. Harris gives her a flier for the upcoming ACORN-sponsored sit-in, set to take place on a bridge that crosses the Industrial Canal into the Lower Ninth. The group is demanding that residents at least be allowed to view their property and salvage what belongings they can. "We're going to make them let us go in," she says.

ACORN, which has temporarily moved its national offices from New Orleans to Baton Rouge, is part of a growing number of activist groups that are working to organize Hurricane Katrina evacuees and help them find roles in the rebuilding of their communities. Shortly after the hurricane struck, Harris was bunking down in the Lamar-Dixon Expo Center shelter in Gonzales, Louisiana, when she received a text message from ACORN. The group helped her find an apartment for an extended family that includes both preschoolers and Harris's 83-year-old grandmother.

Now Harris visits shelters, trailer parks and other sites to organize evacuees. She also traveled to Washington to meet with Congressional leaders and participate in a press conference with House Democratic leader Nancy Pelosi. "This is like therapy for me," Harris says, hurrying across a gravel lot to speak with another trailer-park resident.

In addition to the Lower Nine (as its called here) action, ACORN's activities include Wednesday meetings in Baton Rouge that usually attract about seventy-five evacuees. In mid-October the organization launched a new Hurricane Survivors Association. ACORN's most ambitious effort is scheduled for November 7 and 8, when the group will host a conference on the reconstruction of New Orleans, bringing fifty experts in fields such as urban planning and the environment together with fifty evacuated residents for a series of discussions. These discussions will be teleconferenced across the United States to cities with large concentrations of evacuees. The goal is to arm evacuees with information and to help them find entry points into a reconstruction debate that currently seems as confused as the post-Katrina rescue operation.

"Everyone is talking right now without any plan," says ACORN founder Wade Rathke, who's displaced from his own residence in New Orleans. "I certainly don't have the answers to some issues. I don't know the future of the Ninth Ward. But what I'm certain of is that the voices of people who live in New Orleans are currently being left out of the discussion, and they've got to be at the center of it."

That's also the aim of the Survivors Leadership Group, a Houston-based assembly of evacuated community leaders organized in the wake of Hurricane Katrina by The Metropolitan

Organization (TMO), a group affiliated with the Industrial Areas Foundation network. Renee Barrios, the Foundation's lead organizer in Houston, recalls a Labor Day meeting when the distinction between treating Katrina evacuees as victims and as potential leaders became especially pronounced. On that day, she says, Oprah Winfrey and other celebrities were appearing in the Astrodome, each of them promising aid in voices that boomed over the arena's PA system. Organizers with TMO almost turned around and left, but then decided they should first announce that they were looking for evacuees who wanted to organize.

A core group of about 100 evacuees met that day. Their first successful action was moving a line of evacuees who were waiting for Red Cross assistance at Houston's Reliant Center out of the stifling heat and into the air-conditioned building. The group also launched a successful petition drive that prompted Houston Mayor Bill White to ask the Federal Communications Commission to restrain cell phone providers from cutting off 504-area phones for nonpayment of bills.

The group also gained a spot in White's "Katrina Working Group," along with police officials, school administrators, city councilors and other local decision-makers. "When the mayor asked us to come to the table," says Barrios, "we said that we'll participate, but we're going to organize. Survivors are going to know best what's going to work and not work."

Christine Stephens, an Industrial Areas Foundation supervising organizer, says the group is working on two fronts: to help evacuees work toward better living conditions in their new communities, and to help those returning to New Orleans have a say in the rebuilding. In Louisiana that means gaining access to the various commissions headed by Governor Kathleen

Blanco and New Orleans Mayor Ray Nagin, as well as getting folks' voices heard in upcoming special legislative sessions.

TMO and ACORN are working on separate tracks toward common goals; neither Rathke nor Barrios seems particularly interested in combining forces. Some coalitions are forming, however. ACORN has teamed with the NAACP, along with the AFL-CIO and other labor groups, to form New Opportunity and Hope, calling attention to worker-related issues during the reconstruction. In New Orleans veteran activists and political consultants have formed two umbrella groups for activists: the People's Hurricane Relief Fund and Oversight Coalition, and the Rebuilding Louisiana Coalition.

Organizing displaced residents to agitate on their own behalf poses unusual challenges. "I call people to tell them about a meeting," says Tanya Harris, "and they say, I'm in Idaho." For Harris, the first step remains getting her old neighbors back to the Lower Nine. As she sees it, that will keep them on the path toward home. Walking through the Baker trailer park, she doesn't hide her disappointment every time she encounters residents who say they're not going back. About half the people she meets tonight tell her this.

"Are you going to return?" she asks a couple from Harvey. "To what?" the man answers blankly. "My apartment? It's gone."

Harris tells them ACORN can help them find housing wherever they land. She takes down their names and phone numbers. On her way back to the car, she says that she knows everyone has tough choices to make, but it's difficult talking to people who are moving on. "Decisions are being made all around us," she says. "I want us to go back to fight."

A Second-Line Revival

by Billy Sothern

[posted online on January 25, 2006]

> "In this place, there's a custom for the funerals of jazz musi-
> cians. The funeral procession parades slowly through the
> streets, followed by a band playing a mournful dirge as it moves
> to the cemetery. Once the casket has been laid in place, the band
> breaks into a joyful 'second line,' symbolizing the triumph of the
> spirit over death. Tonight the Gulf Coast is still coming through
> the dirge, yet we will live to see the second line."
> —GEORGE W. BUSH, September 15, 2005

WORD SPREAD in bars, coffee shops and by way of
New Orleans' independent radio station, WWOZ,
that there was going to be a second line at 10 Saturday morning starting at Sweet Loraine's on Saint Claude Avenue. The
parade was with the Black Men of Labor, who second-line annu-

ally on Labor Day. There were to be two brass bands, The Hot 8 and To Be Continued, a group of teenage musicians.

By the time I arrived at the closed bar, an odd assortment of recently returned city residents were milling about on the sidewalk and the trash-strewn neutral ground. Amid duct-taped refrigerators and piles of moldy sheetrock, residents of the surrounding neighborhoods where the second-line culture has lived for generations watched with anticipation as the pre-parade drama unfolded. Gutter punks, their faces tattooed and pierced, were dressed for a postapocalyptic ball, with girls in tutus and dresses and men in top hats. Middle-aged music aficionados were also mixed into the crowd, wearing vintage "Jazzfest 88" T-shirts that testified to their authentic love of New Orleans' music. The whole scene was under the magnifying glass of 100 cameras and a dozen video cameras, recording the moment for posterity.

One documentarian, in a Yankees hat and with a large movie crew, was especially conspicuous. The storm had blown in Spike Lee, a genuine national celebrity. In a city that is just as eager to revere its own local celebrities—like Mister Quintron, an indie musician and inventor of the Drum Buddy; rock-star celebrity chef Susan Spicer; and the late Ernie K-Doe, singer of the 1960s R&B classic "Mother-in-Law" and self-proclaimed "emperor of the world"—Spike Lee attracted little more attention than the rest of the many cameramen as he worked on his new documentary, *When the Levees Broke*. No one had come to Sweet Loraine's to gawk at stars other than the dozen or so men in yellow shirts who were set to perform their distinctive dance up and down New Orleans' streets.

As we waited for the parade to start, an off-the-cuff press conference began, with cameras converging around the dapper men and people asking questions about the meaning of the second line after the storm. As New Orleanians are rarely at a loss for words these days in explaining their plight and the significance of their lives and culture (nothing like being left for dead by the rest of your country to make you realize that you have to speak up for yourself), Fred Johnson, one of the founders of the thirteen-year-old Second-Line Club, wearing a black fedora and dark glasses, responded at length, linking New Orleans' black cultural traditions to those of his ancestors, who were slaves in Louisiana. "Slaves created gumbo from the scraps off the table out of what no one else wanted," he said. "The big house didn't know what the little house was doin', but when they found out, it became a cuisine." He enunciated "cuisine" with slight mockery and derision but also with understanding—as, of course, who wouldn't want gumbo?

Not everyone was eager to listen to talking, though. Interrupting the monologue, a lanky middle-aged black man announced, "I came here to dance! Where's the music at?" He was soon placated by the booming moan of Bennie "Big Peter" Pete tuning his tuba. A heavy black woman with a tiny Nike backpack and big gold earrings, with a faint tattoo of an M on her hand, was ecstatic at the sound: "Bring me back home. Waah, waaah, waah, waaah. I been waiting to hear that. I been hearing it in my sleep."

As The Hot 8 tuned up, the Black Men of Labor disappeared into Sweet Loraine's, and the excitement of the promise of real New Orleans culture after months in the monoculture of Jackson, Houston and Pensacola spread among the crowd.

The Hot 8 began playing "E Flat Blues," and tears came to people's eyes as they gathered around outside, waiting for the second-liners to emerge from Sweet Loraine's. Then each player burst through the doors, one by one, like the hometown team coming onto the basketball court at the beginning of the game. Each man, dressed in the same yellow-and-black outfit, expressed an individual character coming through the darkened doors. Some sauntered, some strutted, and one particularly inspired dancer walked and danced in a squat with his butt almost on the sidewalk. Cheers for each of them were barely discernible over the loud brass.

When the last man was through, we began to walk, en masse, down Saint Claude Avenue, a street that runs through the now famously devastated Ninth Ward. The parade turned up Saint Bernard Avenue, and the brown, chest-high waterline became evident on the facades of people's old wood-frame shotgun houses.

As the band finished up "Paul Barbarin's Second Line," the dancers quickly headed into Mickey's Next Stop Bar, followed by about fifty paraders, all wanting a quick beer. It was unclear whether the bar just happened to be open at 11:15 on the parade route or whether these were normal hours in this near-vacant, crumbling neighborhood. But certainly, the few late-morning drinkers inside must have been surprised at all the company.

As sometimes happens here, we got sidetracked at the bar. This time the delay was justified by the fact that two critical components of the second line—beer and hot sausage po' boys, typically sold from the beds of pickup trucks following the parade—were absent.

The band got going again with a slow dirge as the parade resumed slowly up Saint Bernard into Tremé, one of the oldest black neighborhoods in America, where free people of color built homes in the mid-eighteenth century. We passed the neighborhood grocery store, the old Circle Grocery, which had become an emblem of New Orleans' post-Katrina chaos and was shown beneath deep water with nauseating frequency on CNN from the elevated interstate that runs next to it. The sad music captured the feeling so many of us had as evacuees looking at elements of our everyday lives turned upside down and projected to a national audience to tell the story of this terrible natural disaster.

The band, however, refused to dwell on this mood for long and commenced a rousing "I'll Fly Away," just as it passed under the interstate. With the sound trapped beneath the highway, the acoustics exploded. The band stopped marching and played even harder, as everyone cheered ecstatically.

When the song ended, the parade turned onto Claiborne Avenue, which runs under the highway and which served for generations as the center of commerce and social life for Tremé. It had been a wide neutral ground and once had elegant oaks under which families often picnicked. But the oaks were cut down and the neutral ground was paved for parking when the highway was built above Claiborne Avenue in the 1960s as part of a backward "urban development" plan. Recently, the oaks have reappeared as murals on the massive, concrete cylinders that support the highway, providing imagined shade to the many persistent families who still picnic there on lawn chairs, just as their great-grandparents did.

On the corner of Claiborne and Columbus, the parade made a left and lingered for a moment under the interstate again before the band and the Second Liners scurried over to

Antoinette K-Doe. She was sitting on the corner in front of the Mother-in-Law Lounge, which she opened with her late husband as a venue for New Orleans music and tradition. Even before K-Doe's death, in 2001, it was a museum of artifacts from his career—it even contained a life-size K-Doe in one of his old '60s outfits. Almost all of the many images that adorned the walls featured K-Doe—with rare exceptions, including a painting of Christ. Since K-Doe's passing, Antoinette has been more open about the fact that the lounge is, and always was, a shrine to her legendary spouse.

Miss Antoinette is a revered figure in New Orleans among musicians of all stripes, from brass bands to indie rockers. In addition to her years as K-Doe's "wife, his manager, his secretary, his bartender, everything," as she described it to me recently, she is also a cousin of Lee Dorsey, the writer and singer of the New Orleans anthem and '60s R&B hit "Ya-Ya," as well as a singer and dancer in her own right.

All of the musicians and dancers stopped to check in with Miss Antoinette, offering condolences for the extensive flood damage that the lounge and K-Doe's old black limo suffered in the storm. She remained smiling, optimistic and proud in all of her exchanges as she sat against the bright-colored murals of musicians on the exterior cinderblock walls of the lounge. In sharp contrast, everyone could easily see past Miss Antoinette, through the doorway, into the gray and gutted lounge. As empress of all of this, Miss Antoinette greeted Spike Lee as she did everyone else, and posed with him for a picture taken by one of his crew, seemingly for him to hang on his office wall.

We got going again, down Columbus Street, a block that three months earlier had been an open-air drug market but that had since been abandoned to flooded cars and garbage, including a flood-darkened Ziploc bag with "pickled lips" handwritten on the white label. On the next block down, in the fenced-in schoolyard of the McDonough 35 High School, the parade approached a group of young black men in orange jumpsuits with "OPP" stenciled in black block letters on the chest. These men, prisoners of the Orleans Parish Prison, which only three months earlier had left hundreds of men to drown in their cells in the rising water, ran to the high, chain-link fence and danced to the rhythm of their home, their neighborhoods, with their fists in the air. Cute women in pigtails and handmade "Make Levees, Not War" T-shirts danced in the sunny street on the other side of the fence, framed against the burned-out shell of an old Creole cottage.

The Hot 8, no strangers to urban criminal justice, stopped and began a special performance for the men behind the fence, playing an impromptu "Let My People Go." This act of solidarity reminded me of the band's own loss when a year earlier, only about five blocks from the schoolyard, The Hot 8's trombone player, "Shotgun" Joe Williams, was killed by police. (Though the media made much of his nickname in justifying the shooting of this unarmed man, anyone familiar with local jazz could explain that "shotgun" is a colloquialism for the trombone.) While the band was scheduled to play to a mostly white, upper-middle-class crowd in the French Quarter later in the day, it is unlikely that audience received the same kind of passionate and personal performance that The Hot 8 gave for the men in the orange jumpsuits.

The parade wrapped up its tour of the Tremé in front of the Back Street Museum, a museum of New Orleans' black cultural history in the shadow of the old Saint Augustine Church, where generations of Tremé musicians were baptized. The staff had made red beans and rice, which they gave to the dancers and musicians, and then to everyone else. Some activists circulated a petition for Category Five hurricane levee protection, and others informed the crowd of a march the following week to protest the city's lack of commitment to rebuild poor neighborhoods. They passed out fliers with the South African antiapartheid anthem "Nothing Without Us Is for Us" providing the details. Everyone seemed optimistic and at home, and unlike almost any other place where New Orleanians congregate, no one talked at all about moving away.

We had, for a moment, lived up to the President's prediction and triumphed over the spirit of death with a second line through a city that had been left to die as he watched from the big house, while his wife no doubt explained to him that what we have down here is "culture."

Let the People Rebuild New Orleans

by Naomi Klein

[from the September 26, 2005 issue]

ON SEPTEMBER 4, six days after Katrina hit, I saw the first glimmer of hope. "The people of New Orleans will not go quietly into the night, scattering across this country to become homeless in countless other cities while federal relief funds are funneled into rebuilding casinos, hotels, chemical plants. . . . We will not stand idly by while this disaster is used as an opportunity to replace our homes with newly built mansions and condos in a gentrified New Orleans."

The statement came from Community Labor United, a coalition of low-income groups in New Orleans. It went on to demand that a committee made up of evacuees "oversee FEMA, the Red Cross and other organizations collecting resources on behalf of our people. . . . We are calling for evacuees from our community to actively participate in the rebuilding of New Orleans."

LET THE PEOPLE REBUILD NEW ORLEANS

It's a radical concept: The $10.5 billion released by Congress and the $500 million raised by private charities doesn't actually belong to the relief agencies or the government; it belongs to the victims. The agencies entrusted with the money should be accountable to them. Put another way, the people Barbara Bush tactfully described as "underprivileged anyway" just got very rich.

Except relief and reconstruction never seem to work like that. When I was in Sri Lanka six months after the tsunami, many survivors told me that the reconstruction was victimizing them all over again. A council of the country's most prominent businesspeople had been put in charge of the process, and they were handing the coast over to tourist developers at a frantic pace. Meanwhile, hundreds of thousands of poor fishing people were still stuck in sweltering inland camps, patrolled by soldiers with machine guns and entirely dependent on relief agencies for food and water. They called reconstruction "the second tsunami."

There are already signs that New Orleans evacuees could face a similarly brutal second storm. Jimmy Reiss, chairman of the New Orleans Business Council, told *Newsweek* that he has been brainstorming about how "to use this catastrophe as a once-in-an-eon opportunity to change the dynamic." The Business Council's wish list is well-known: low wages, low taxes, more luxury condos and hotels. Before the flood, this highly profitable vision was already displacing thousands of poor African-Americans: While their music and culture was for sale in an increasingly corporatized French Quarter (where only 4.3 percent of residents are black), their housing developments were being torn down. "For white tourists and businesspeople, New Orleans' reputation is 'a great place to have a vacation but

don't leave the French Quarter or you'll get shot,' " Jordan Flaherty, a New Orleans-based labor organizer told me the day after
he left the city by boat. "Now the developers have their big
chance to disperse the obstacle to gentrification—poor people."

Here's a better idea: New Orleans could be reconstructed by
and for the very people most victimized by the flood. Schools
and hospitals that were falling apart before could finally have
adequate resources; the rebuilding could create thousands of
local jobs and provide massive skills training in decent paying
industries. Rather than handing over the reconstruction to the
same corrupt elite that failed the city so spectacularly, the
effort could be led by groups like Douglass Community Coalition. Before the hurricane this remarkable assembly of parents,
teachers, students and artists was trying to reconstruct the city
from the ravages of poverty by transforming Frederick Douglass
Senior High School into a model of community learning. They
have already done the painstaking work of building consensus
around education reform. Now that the funds are flowing,
shouldn't they have the tools to rebuild every ailing public
school in the city?

For a people's reconstruction process to become a reality (and
to keep more contracts from going to Halliburton), the evacuees must be at the center of all decision-making. According
to Curtis Muhammad of Community Labor United, the disaster's starkest lesson is that African-Americans cannot count
on any level of government to protect them. "We had no caretakers," he says. That means the community groups that do
represent African-Americans in Louisiana and Mississippi—
many of which lost staff, office space and equipment in the
flood—need our support now. Only a massive injection of

cash and volunteers will enable them to do the crucial work of organizing evacuees—currently scattered through forty-one states—into a powerful political constituency. The most pressing question is where evacuees will live over the next few months. A dangerous consensus is building that they should collect a little charity, apply for a job at the Houston Wal-Mart and move on. Muhammad and CLU, however, are calling for the right to return: they know that if evacuees are going to have houses and schools to come back to, many will need to return to their home states and fight for them.

These ideas are not without precedent. When Mexico City was struck by a devastating earthquake in 1985, the state also failed the people: poorly constructed public housing crumbled and the army was ready to bulldoze buildings with survivors still trapped inside. A month after the quake 40,000 angry refugees marched on the government, refusing to be relocated out of their neighborhoods and demanding a "Democratic Reconstruction." Not only were 50,000 new dwellings for the homeless built in a year; the neighborhood groups that grew out of the rubble launched a movement that is challenging Mexico's traditional power holders to this day.

And the people I met in Sri Lanka have grown tired of waiting for the promised relief. Some survivors are now calling for a People's Planning Commission for Post-Tsunami Recovery. They say the relief agencies should answer to them; it's their money, after all.

The idea could take hold in the United States, and it must. Because there is only one thing that can compensate the victims of this most human of natural disasters, and that is what has been denied them throughout: power. It will be a long and difficult battle, but New Orleans' evacuees should draw strength from the knowledge that they are no longer poor people; they are rich people who have been temporarily locked out of their bank accounts.

Those wanting to donate to a people's reconstruction can make checks out to the Vanguard Public Foundation, 383 Rhode Island St., Suite 301, San Francisco, CA 94103. Checks should be earmarked "People's Hurricane Fund."

New Orleans: Raze or Rebuild?

by Christian Parenti

[posted online on September 12, 2005]

THE WATER IN the lower Ninth Ward is thickening into a glassy, fetid slick as the gasoline, oil, solvents and sewage from thousands of submerged vehicles and homes leaches out. Some rescue crews can stay out on their boats for only an hour before getting light-headed. The water's blue-black sheen casts back an almost mocking mirror image of the horrible devastation and incongruously beautiful blue sky above.

A tour from Houston to Gulfport and into New Orleans for several days revealed not only this type of weird physical destruction but also a landscape of raw and tangled emotions, ranging from open fantasies of an impending race war to inspiring, ad hoc experiments in interracial mutual aid and grassroots organizing. This mix of the best and worst in American culture suggests the widely divergent political possibilities left in Katrina's wake. The storm could become an excuse to banish the

African-American poor in the interests of the private redevelopment of New Orleans, or the city could become the geographic center of a progressive program of urban revitalization.

In the lower Ninth Ward, controlled breaks by the Army Corps of Engineers have dropped the water by several feet, opening an archipelago of scum-encrusted islands that can be navigated by way of partially open streets. Late in the second week of the disaster a colleague and I made our way through this eerie and desolate maze.

Though the area is routinely designated a ghetto, the homes of the Ninth Ward are mostly beautiful, century-old capes and bungalows, some with ornate wooden detailing reminiscent of old homes in the San Francisco Bay Area. "They'll have to bulldoze it all," says a visiting New York City cop, surveying the damage from inside an NYPD van.

Is that option—the right's much-touted tabula rasa—inevitable? "They don't have to tear all these down," says Joe Peters, a Ninth Ward tier repairman. "Under that siding, that's all cypress frames and barge board." Peters seems to think that the more solid homes of the Ninth Ward can be saved. Increasingly the holdouts here see the mandatory evacuation order as part of a huge land grab.

I track down Mike Howell, a *Nation* reader I'd met several days before. "Yeah, this could be their dream come true," he says. "Get rid of all the poor African-Americans and turn the place into Disneyland." After camping on Howell's roof, my colleague and I leave him and his wife our extra water and gas and push on.

At Kajun's, one of only two bars open at the end of last week, a bacchanalian, slap-happy air prevails among the handful of drunk and adrenaline-pumped patrons. A big man with a ponytail is weeping—he just put down his dog because it was biting everyone. A wide-eyed young woman named Caroline is changing the bandage on a dog-bite victim and talking a mile a minute. "I am a massage therapist, but I am not licensed. I am giving garlic and herbs to everyone, even the soldiers."

Outside, a man slips two bottles of cognac into the back seat of a police vehicle. The officer isn't harassing the patrons to leave. Someone brings him a big plastic cup of something iced.

"The evacuation order is just trying to get out the criminal element," says the cop in the classic flat, nasal Yat accent common to the Irish- and Italian-Americans who make up much of the city's white population. He explains how the military is mapping the city for holdouts using helicopters with infrared, and how troops on the ground mark the suspect building with a system of Xs and checks, a code that indicates to the police how many people are inside. The cop finishes his drink, shakes a few hands and rolls off.

Facilitating the tabula rasa agenda is an increasingly militaristic attitude that borders on boyish fantasy and seems to pervade the numerous federal SWAT teams, out-of-town cops, private security forces, civilian volunteers and even journalists. There are exceptions:

The young soldiers of the 82nd Airborne and First Cavalry seem much less caught up in it and are quite generous with their ice and MREs.

When an APC full of federal marshals passes deep in the Ninth Ward, a journalist in a camo floppy hat riding with them glares at me and demands, "Who are you with?" For a second I think he's a cop.

Downtown, a man on a bicycle wearing a pistol and carrying a medical bag says he's an emergency medical technician. "I had to shoot one guy in the arm," the man explains. "He was going for the bag. They think it's full of drugs."

Elsewhere, two vehicle convoys from Blackwater USA—one of the biggest mercenary firms operating in Iraq—cruise the deserted city, their guns trained on rooftops ready for snipers, who have recently shot at a cell-tower repair crew.

It seems the rescue effort is turning into an urban war game: An imaginary domestic version of the total victory that eludes America in Baghdad will be imposed here, on New Orleans. It's almost as if the Tigris—rather than the Mississippi—had flooded the city. The place feels like a sick theme park—Macho World—where cops, mercenaries, journalists and weird volunteers of all sorts are playing out a relatively safe version of their militaristic fantasies about Armageddon and the cleansing iron fist.

GOD'S WRATH IN GULFPORT

IN GULFPORT, MISSISSIPPI, God's wrath hath smitten the evil gaming industry. All the giant floating multi-story casinos have washed away—and much of their cash is unaccounted for. So, too, have all the houses on the beach been wiped out. An area two blocks from the beach is cordoned off because the shore is strewn with tons of rotting chicken and pork from a grounded freighter. Perhaps that cordon is also protecting the casinos' cash.

At a shuttered gas station, I meet the young white night

watchman, Joseph. He owns a seven-foot-long Monitor lizard and is going to great lengths to keep her warm now that the power is down. "I have my plan for evacuation," he says. "Those people in New Orleans shoulda too, but if you say that, then you're a racist."

Later it comes out that Joseph thinks New Orleans is a cesspool that should be filled with even more water, that he doesn't like Vietnamese people and that he's licensed to carry a gun at all times. "I tell you, we're on the verge of another Civil War in this country."

A white woman pulls in to buy cigarettes. "I think New Orleans is a satanic city," she says earnestly. "I mean, I am not super-religious, but it's a horrible place full of very satanic people." She thinks voodoo and Mardi Gras might have something to do with Katrina's path.

Trying to get gas north of Lake Pontchartrain, back in Louisiana, we pull in to a cops-only refueling depot and chat with a producer from Universal Studios in Florida who is now a volunteer parking attendant for the rescue effort. He's red with sunburn, fidgety and sweaty, his lingo laced with military jargon.

"My orders are to secure this area," he says. "The situation is still pretty volatile here—there are a lot of evacuees from New Orleans around." He nods to the woods as if Charlie is out there on the proverbial tree line. "I am trying to locate a truckload of NYPD ammunition that went missing." Everything about him says this is war. "You guys be careful out there." Gun shops in Baton Rouge are reporting sales of up to a thousand a day.

Outside a Red Cross shelter in Covington, there is a softer version of this siege mentality. When I interview some African-American evacuees, no less than four different white middle-class Red Cross staff intervene at various points, once even attempting to have me evicted from the area by police. In paternalistic tones, they explain to the black people I am talking with that newspapers and magazines do not give aid.

"Yes, ma'am, I know," says a woman named Raven. "I want the whole world to hear my story." And the stories they tell are harrowing.

A heavy-set older woman named Rosie Lee Riford is on the verge of tears. "I am so worried. I feel like killing myself," she says. Her grown son, who uses a wheelchair due to a childhood gunshot wound, refused to leave the Saint Downs housing project. She was forced to leave without him as the storm took aim at New Orleans. Now that neighborhood is flooded. "I never hurt anybody or did any wrong. I just keep asking God, Why? Why'd you do this?"

For Latino immigrants, the situation can be even worse. A Nicaraguan house painter named Juan tells me he will have to go home to Managua because he has lost everything: car, apartment, the business where he worked. He says the Red Cross cannot register him for benefits, so he eats at Latino churches. He bravely holds back tears.

Not far from the Red Cross is a group from Veterans for Peace, who came here from Camp Casey in Crawford, Texas, and who are now coordinating a large-scale supply depot and distribution center. At the Vets' Internet tent sits Tenshenia Downs, a young, well-organized mother from East New Orleans. She is trying to find her relatives and set up housing in Atlanta. She spent a day on her roof with her three kids and was then evacuated by a National Guard flatboat and taken to the Superdome.

"It was like a prison," she says. "It was hell. They had pedophiles up in there. People living like animals." She recounts the backed-up toilets, urine-flooded halls, the elderly near death, the fistfights, panic, lack of food and limited water.

"They wouldn't let us leave," she continues. "But when I heard about the third rape, I just took my three kids and went. We waded through that water to I-10 and walked over the river to Gretna." From Gretna she walked and hitched rides with truckers and "a real nice white couple" here to Covington. "I lost it all: everything in my house and a new car, no insurance." And the beauty spa where she worked, Bella Donna, is gone.

She says she'll try and start over in Atlanta. Bizarrely, there is no Red Cross or FEMA clearinghouse of information yet established; instead, Ms. Downs is pointed to the MoveOn.org Web site for housing and job postings in Atlanta.

GRACE AND GENEROSITY IN HOUSTON

AT THE HOUSTON Astrodome, the stereotype of white America's worst nightmare has arrived: a wave of black people from some of the nation's worst ghettos. And, surprise, surprise, it's not so bad.

On the sterile manicured lawns and the sidewalks of the sprawling shopping plaza around Reliant Center, hundreds of young dudes and well-dressed ladies from the Ninth Ward, East New Orleans and other desperately poor and excluded neighborhoods stroll around peacefully.

The relief effort here is far from perfect and involves only some 11,000 people, but it is one of the most functional pieces of the response. The people of Houston have welcomed the evacuees with grace and generosity. Everyone here is getting tetanus shots and other basic healthcare, and they have debit cards (most are only good for a few hundred dollars, not the $2,000 usually cited in the press). And at some point in their stay, the evacuees in the Astrodome each get to spend a week in a hotel, to have some privacy, comfort and solid rest. Many are being successfully placed in more long-term housing and even set up with jobs. Their children will be entering schools that in many cases are far better than the disastrous system they left in New Orleans.

Looking out at the scene, I can't help but be moved by its peaceful contrast to the flood-zone militarism. Nor is the so-called "culture of poverty" much in evidence. What is so striking here is not the role of culture but the role of opportunities, services and money. When the poor are treated with some modicum of respect and given a few resources, the social benefits are immediately apparent. When offered the chance, most of them rebuild their lives.

Meanwhile, in Baton Rouge, Bush-connected firms like the Shaw Group, Bechtel and Halliburton are lining up to get big portions of the $62 billion in federal money that will soon flood the storm region. The fact that some of these companies had been convicted of defrauding the federal government in the past, are under investigation again for corruption in Iraq and were once banned from federal contracting due to unethical practices has not stopped the process. Many of the people here at the Astrodome, aware of the money headed to the region, say they too would like the chance to help reconstruct and shape their city.

A "New" New Deal

by William Greider

[from the October 3, 2005 issue]

T HE CATASTROPHE, AS many seem to grasp, is one of those big moments that jolt public consciousness and alter the course of national history. I would go further and describe it as an exclamation point that marks a dramatic breakdown for the reigning right-wing orthodoxy, the beginning of its retreat and eventual demise. This by no means insures the restoration of progressive alternatives, but events have at least reopened the argument conservatives thought they had won.

A profound political question is suddenly on the table: Must the country continue to give precedence to private financial gain and market determinism over human lives and broad public values? Or shall we now undertake a radical restoration on behalf of society and people? New Orleans, strange exception though it seems, is actually an extreme microcosm of the nation's general afflictions and social inequities. It's the place where reform politics can launch its long-deferred counteroffensive.

The conservative mindset is flummoxed by these tragic new circumstances. Republican ideologues acquired governing power by promising to liberate Americans from the government's intrusive powers, but they succeeded all too well. If "market forces" are allowed to design the recovery program, much of New Orleans and environs will be plowed up (think no-bid contracts for Halliburton and Bechtel) and reduced to a theme park for hot jazz, good restaurants and grubby jobs.

Newt Gingrich, always a reliable bellwether for the right-wing zeitgeist, is preaching that the right must change its tune "quickly" or face big losses. The old politics—provoking culture wars about "moral values"—will no longer suffice, he explained in a memo circulated among Republicans and the press. The new politics is about "performance," in which GOP government has to deliver. But while Gingrich's rhetoric is different, his ideas are the same old, same old. He urges George W. Bush to create a huge tax-free zone along the Gulf Coast where business enterprise will be subsidized and the oil industry relieved of meddlesome environmental regulation. The President's first noble gesture after the flood was to cut wages for construction workers on public projects.

More encouraging evidence of changed politics comes from the left. Some bold Democrats are doing what they haven't dared to do for many years, even decades: They are invoking their New Deal legacy and applying its liberal operating assumptions to the present crisis. In the totality of the Gulf Coast destruction, the economy and the society have been collapsed. As New Dealers understood, you cannot fix one without fixing the other. And only the federal government has the resources and authority to lead such a complex undertaking.

Senator Edward Kennedy calls for a "Gulf Coast Regional Redevelopment Authority," modeled after FDR's Tennessee Valley Authority, to lead the rebuilding. Former Senator John Edwards proposes a vast new jobs program, patterned after the New Deal's Works Progress Administration (WPA) and Civilian Conservation Corps (CCC), in which the displaced and the poor are hired at living wages to clean up and rebuild their devastated communities. In the week after Katrina, Representatives Dennis Kucinich and Stephanie Tubbs Jones swiftly rounded up eighty-eight House co-sponsors, including some from Mississippi and Louisiana, for a similar initiative.

As the dimensions of this challenge become clearer, reformers will discover other New Deal models they can emulate and adapt to present circumstances. For instance, in the 1930s Roosevelt's Reconstruction Finance Corporation was a central player in rebuilding the industrial economy, because it acted like a public-spirited investment banker empowered to channel startup capital to collapsed companies, provide temporary protection from creditors and impose equitable terms on how the private firms relate to social priorities. This time cities and schools need similar help.

The government, meanwhile, must quickly become the employer of last resort across the region. Neither local school systems nor small-business employers can recover unless their communities have a large, reliable base of wage incomes—that is, government-financed jobs to sustain customers and taxpayers. You can't rebuild homes without tools and materials or temporary relief from mortgage defaults. You can't reopen schools if their tax base is gone. You can't prevent poor people from sliding back into desperate conditions unless government creates ladders of upward mobility.

Recognizing such social-economic connections was the essence of New Deal innovation. Serious politicians need to jump-start their imaginations. This born-again New Deal spirit isn't backward-looking but instead can seize the opportunity to address grave issues—such as the myriad ecological dangers spawned by our hydrocarbon economy—that status-quo politics neglects, like the New Orleans levees.

This new ferment is only just beginning, but the crisis is young, and the hunger for big reform is rapidly gaining momentum. The media haven't paid much attention so far because the New Deal proposals probably sound like historic relics. But the aptness of the ideas—aggressive government intervention, integrated across many fronts—will become clearer to people if Democrats re-educate the electorate. That re-education can begin if progressives first provoke a big argument among Democrats themselves. What do they now believe about government's obligations to society? This is a good fight to have and, besides, intramural political spats are always newsworthy. This one will be substantive as well. Terrible events have handed Democrats the material for a strong and enduring governing agenda.

GEORGE BUSH, MEET "Dr. New Deal." Reactionary Republicans loathed FDR and sneered at his corny slogans, while he wickedly ridiculed them in return. The voters understood his spirit and forgave the mistakes. They laughed with him and loved him for caring.

History Lessons

by Katrina vanden Heuvel

[posted online on September 8, 2005]

NEW ORLEANS IS destroyed, the Gulf Coast's infrastructure is in tatters and tens of thousands of citizens are without jobs as gas prices nationwide rise to record levels. Television sets brought the destruction into all of our homes. But this White House seemed unable to grasp the misery unfolding before its own eyes.

Instead, President Bush treated the disaster as if he were a loutish frat boy when he joked to Americans that he had had good times partying in New Orleans as a young man and hoped in the near future to be able to sit on Senator Trent Lott's rebuilt porch in Mississippi.

But to really understand what went wrong with the Administration's shameful response, we need to look beyond Bush's blame-the-other, pass-the-buck and who-gives-a-*@* attitude.

The Administration's ineptitude, as *New York Times* columnist Paul Krugman put it, was "a consequence of ideological hostility to the very idea of using government to serve the public good."

The government's failure was the result not of "simple incompetence" in the Administration but "of a campaign by most Republicans and too many Democrats to systematically vilify the role of government in American life," *Los Angeles Times* columnist Robert Scheer argued. And as the *Financial Times* observed, "For the past quarter-century in Washington . . . U.S. politics has been dominated by the conviction that what was wrong with America would be solved by getting government off the people's backs"—an attitude that contributed to the criminal inaction on the part of the federal government.

INDEED, YOU COULD see what the dog-eat-dog, antigovernment philosophy of the far right has reaped in the bloated bodies and raw sewage in New Orleans's flooded streets.

That philosophy has attained new power under President Bush. While the Louisiana Army Corps of Engineers proposed $18 billion in projects that would have shored up the protective levees, improved flood control and perhaps prevented last week's breaches in the levees' walls, none of these projects were funded. Instead, the White House cut the Corps' budget and actually proposed a further 20 percent cut in 2006.

Which raises the question: What steps should we take to repair the breach that has become so apparent in our social fabric?

Here's one answer: Let's seize this moment by launching a

twenty-first-century New Deal—with programs modeled after the Works Progress Administration, updated for these times. Why?

A modernized version of the WPA would help our nation to rebuild New Orleans and Mississippi's Gulf Coast, and repair the racial and class divides that we saw in such dramatic relief these past few days. It would rebuild and improve our nation's public infrastructure and (hopefully) alter the terms of our political discourse in the years ahead.

After all, Roosevelt's New Deal was so much more than simply a vehicle for providing economic relief to citizens in need. It gave Americans a sense of solidarity, a new social contract, as well as the chance to go to work. It also helped bring the country's infrastructure into the twentieth century.

Take a moment to consider these statistics: The WPA, according to historian William Leuchtenburg, "built or improved more than 2,500 hospitals, 5,900 school buildings, 1,000 airport landing fields, and nearly 13,000 playgrounds."

When the hurricane happened the poverty rate in New Orleans stood at 28 percent—more than double the national average. Fully half the children of Louisiana now live in poverty, the second-highest child poverty rate in the country (its neighbor, Mississippi, is number one). And as if to underscore the poverty of our politics, the same week the hurricane devastated the poorest regions the Census Bureau released a report that found the number of Americans living in poverty has climbed again—for the fourth straight year under President Bush.

African-Americans, who are two-thirds of the city's population, suffered the most in the hurricane's wake. As Professor Mark Naison wrote in a letter circulating on the Web, this event is nothing short of "a humanitarian challenge of unprecedented proportions."

It showed "how deeply divided our nation is and how far our social fabric has been strained" by the Iraq war and by "policies which have widened the gap between rich and poor."

A post-New Orleans WPA could help to spark a new and desperately needed moral struggle for economic rights. It could provide jobs to Louisiana and Mississippi's poor and promote the goals of equality, justice and economic opportunity across American society.

(Bush's approach, in contrast, favors cronyism. Last week, [September 1st, 2005] Halliburton's stock hit a fifty-two-week high, presumably because Dick Cheney's former colleagues may reap the benefits of this tragedy securing government contracts to rebuild the Gulf Coast. Bush's approach has been a complete failure for the poor, elderly and largely African-American population of New Orleans.)

A WPA-style program could also begin to address the related crisis of the inner cities—a crisis that, as the Center for American Progress points out, this Administration has contributed to—as it has "repeatedly slashed job training [to the tune of more than $500 million] and vocational education programs."

The Milton Eisenhower Foundation has argued that the federal government should fund 1.25 million public-sector inner-city jobs. (Its Web site lays out a series of "what work" programs.)

We need a twenty-first-century WPA to restore the infrastructure not only in Louisiana and Mississippi, but in every state in America. As Representative Dennis Kucinich said this past week, the task ahead that is required to rebuild New

Orleans includes a need for "new levees, new roads, bridges, libraries, schools, colleges and universities and . . . all public institutions, including hospitals." The government's highest priority should be on affordable housing and public infrastructure, not on casinos and luxury hotels, which skew development and contribute to environmental degradation.

We're "the only major industrial society that is not . . . renewing and expanding its public infrastructure," the Eisenhower Foundation reported. Instead of pork barrel spending on absurd bridges like "Don Young's Way" in Alaska, let's have the federal government spend our money wisely to modernize our hospitals, highways, universities and other institutions.

Senator Kennedy said in a Senate floor speech this week [September 8, 2005] that "we can't just fix the hole in the roof. We need to rebuild the whole foundation." He proposed establishing "a New Orleans and Gulf Coast Redevelopment Authority modeled after the Tennessee Valley Authority in its heyday." His good idea is to "plan, help fund and coordinate for the reconstruction of that damaged region."

Finally, we must seek to upend twenty-five years of rightwing political dogma that is responsible for what went wrong in responding to this disaster.

We need a new politics of shared sacrifice and a renewed commitment to a politics of shared prosperity—with a federal government playing a vital role in creating a fairer, more just, full-employment economy. These proposals are common sense ideas; how could they be considered heretical in the hurricane's wake?

This is a moment ripe to reshape Americans' view of government. A twenty-first-century version of the WPA would halt the dismantling and begin the rebuilding of our nation's communities, of lives enmeshed in deep poverty and squalor, and provide some hope that the horrific abandonment by government of thousands of citizens will be an aberration, not a nightmarish portent of what lies ahead.

Visionaries Wanted

by Nicholas von Hoffman

[posted online on September 19, 2005]

IN THE SPIRIT of top-down government, talk abounds about the appointment of a czar, kaiser or gauleiter to run the reconstruction of the Gulf communities destroyed by Hurricane Katrina. The name of Jack Welch, former General Electric CEO, is mentioned. He'd be perfect, famous, as he is, for his considerate treatment of subordinates.

The hundreds of thousands of low- and moderate-income people whose lives have been blasted are not heard from. Nor will they be, scattered and unorganized as they are. If reconstruction continues in the direction it has been going, the displaced will get what they are given and can start practicing how to look grateful for it.

These people could be organized to have a voice in their own destinies. The Industrial Areas Foundation, which has organized scores of low- and moderate-income communities across the country, including in Texas and Mississippi, has the organizers with the skills and experience to mobilize marooned and powerless people. With organization comes democratic decision-making.

The rebuilt communities do not have to resemble penitentiaries or other forms of government housing. There are architects and developers who have made it a specialty to work with limited-income communities to design and build what people want. Among them are Telesis Corporation of Washington, D.C., the brainchild of Marilyn Melkonian, with many low-income home developments to her credit. In Chicago, there is Archeworks, founded by architect Stanley Tigerman, who, with his wife, Margaret McCurry, a gifted architect also, has a long history of working with community groups. The National Organization of Minority Architects is assembling resources and expertise to devote to the rebuilding effort.

Among the architects and designers qualified by experience and prizewinning results to collaborate with grassroots organizations are: Urban Design Associates in Pittsburgh; Calthorpe Associates in Berkeley; Pyatok Architects in Oakland; Moule & Polyzoides Architects and Urbanists in Pasadena; and, in Boston, Goody Clancy.

Grandiose talk aside, in the practical realm the skill, talent and experience is available to take this catastrophe and turn it into a political, social and design marvel. This thing doesn't have to be another hack politician, crony boy, bureaucratic morass that produces more excuses than homes. If a couple of the big foundations, for once in their cunctatious lives, got on this fast, instead of a top-down disaster we could have a bottoms-up triumph.

Prez on the Precipice

by The Editors

[from the October 10, 2005 issue]

TWO-TERM PRESIDENCIES rarely end on the twentieth day of January in the odd year following a national election. Rather, history tells us, they tend to flame out months—sometimes years—before the Oval Office officially changes hands. After a response to Hurricane Katrina that reinforced Americans' doubts about George W. Bush's competence and his caring, and with continuing turns for the worse in Iraq, the President has blundered toward the precipice of a prematurely finished presidency. But as history also tells us, presidencies don't plunge into political free-fall on their own. The opposition party must stoke public resentment and offer convincing alternatives to the Commander in Chief's failed vision.

Bush boosted his sagging approval ratings a bit by tarting up his Gulf Coast reconstruction plans in Franklin Roosevelt drag. But he's facing a revolt within his own party over what some see as an attempt to spend his way out of the doghouse. The danger for Democrats is that the debate over rebuilding New Orleans and the rest of the stricken region could play out as an intramural fight between a "compassionate" President and his fiscally conservative compatriots. That would leave Democrats where they were after the 9/11 terrorist attacks—as hapless allies with a President they are unwilling, or unsure of how, to challenge.

This is no time for such timidity. If Democrats want to get the better of Bush at last, and if they want to advance an agenda that could revitalize their party and their country, they must not get stuck between the Administration and its right flank. They must be blunt about the fact that while it has a big price tag, Bush's response to the Gulf Coast crisis is inadequate and irresponsible. The first step is fighting the President's decision to waive prevailing-wage laws on the Gulf Coast—a giveaway to contractors that denies displaced workers a chance to earn enough to piece their lives back together. Democrats should reject the President's attempts to ease environmental regulations in a region already ecologically devastated. They should back a proposal by Senator Russ Feingold and Representative John Conyers to delay the implementation of bankruptcy "reforms" that will make it tougher for Gulf Coast residents to get back on their feet. And they should launch a frontal assault on the tax policies of an Administration that has starved the government's capacity to provide basic protections and services. That means shooting down the President's proposal to eliminate estate taxes. It also means demanding that Bush be accountable for the $200 billion he has sunk into Iraq, with no end in sight.

At a time when savvy Republicans are starting to put distance between themselves and the President, Democrats have a chance to develop broad coalitions to demand accountability. Not just accountability for the occupation of Iraq and the campaign of calculated deceit that led us to war but for reckless tax cuts, environmental degradation and other domestic disasters this President has ushered in.

But pushing back against Bush's destructive policies is not enough. While Democrats expose and oppose the President's attempt to make the Gulf Coast a laboratory for conservative pet projects and crony capitalism, they must also lay out a full-scale reconstruction plan of their own—a "people's reconstruction" that advances a democratically accountable, economically viable, socially just and environmentally sustainable plan for regional rebuilding. By doing so, Democrats will accomplish something more lasting and important than nudging a faltering President over the precipice. They will identify their party as the credible alternative—the credible leader—it has failed to be for far too long.

FOUR

After the Flood

25 Questions about the Murder of New Orleans

by Mike Davis and Anthony Fontenot

[posted on Tomdispatch.com and Thenation.com on September 30, 2005]

W E RECENTLY SPENT a week in New Orleans and
southern Louisiana interviewing relief workers,
community activists, urban planners, artists and neighborhood
folks. Even as the latest flood waters from Hurricane Rita
recede, the city remains submerged in anger and frustration.

Indeed, the most toxic debris in New Orleans isn't the sinister gray sludge that coats the streets of the historic Creole
neighborhood of Treme or the Lower Ninth Ward but all the
unanswered questions that have accumulated in the wake of so
much official betrayal and hypocrisy. Where outsiders see simple "incompetence" or "failure of leadership," locals are more
inclined to discern deliberate design and planned neglect—the
murder, not the accidental death, of a great city.

In almost random order, here are twenty-five of the urgent
questions that deeply trouble the local people we spoke with.

Until a grand jury or Congressional committee begins to uncover the answers, the moral (as opposed to simply physical) reconstruction of the New Orleans region will remain impossible.

1. Why did the floodwalls along the 17th Street Canal only break on the New Orleans side and not on the Metairie side? Was this the result of neglect and poor maintenance by New Orleans authorities?

2. Who owned the huge barge that was catapulted through the wall of the Industrial Canal, killing hundreds in the Lower Ninth Ward—the most deadly hit-and-run accident in U.S. history?

3. All of New Orleans and St. Bernard Parish east of the Industrial Canal were drowned, except for the Almonaster-Michoud Industrial District along Chef Menteur Highway. Why was industrial land apparently protected by stronger levees than nearby residential neighborhoods?

4. Why did Mayor Ray Nagin, in defiance of his own official disaster plan, delay twelve to twenty-four hours in ordering a mandatory evacuation of the city?

5. Why did Secretary of Homeland Security Michael Chertoff not declare Katrina an "Incident of National Significance" until August 31—thus preventing the full deployment of urgently needed federal resources?

6. Why wasn't the nearby USS *Bataan* immediately sent to the aid of New Orleans? The huge amphibious-landing ship had a state-of-the-art, 600-bed hospital, water and power plants, helicopters, food supplies, and 1,200 sailors eager to join the rescue effort.

7. Similarly, why wasn't the Baltimore-based hospital ship USS *Comfort* ordered to sea until August 31, or the 82nd Airborne Division deployed in New Orleans until September 5?

8. Why does Secretary of Defense Donald Rumsfeld balk at making public his "severe weather execution order" that established the ground rules for the military response to Katrina? Did the Pentagon, as a recent report by the Congressional Research Service suggests, fail to take initiatives within already authorized powers, then attempt to transfer the blame to state and local governments?

9. Why were the more than 350 buses of the New Orleans Regional Transportation Authority—eventually flooded where they were parked—not mobilized to evacuate infirm, poor, and car-less residents?

10. What significance attaches to the fact that the chair of the Transportation Authority, appointed by Mayor Nagin, is Jimmy Reiss, the wealthy leader of the New Orleans Business Council, which has long advocated

a thorough redevelopment of (and cleanup of crime in) the city?

11. Under what authority did Mayor Nagin meet confidentially in Dallas with the "forty thieves"—white business leaders led by Reiss—reportedly to discuss the triaging of poorer black areas and a corporate-led master plan for rebuilding the city?

12. Everyone knows about a famous train called "the City of New Orleans." Why was there no evacuation by rail? Was Amtrak part of the disaster planning? If not, why not?

13. Why were patients at private hospitals like Tulane evacuated by helicopter while their counterparts at the Charity Hospital were left to suffer and die?

14. Was the failure to adequately stock food, water, portable toilets, cots and medicine at the Louisiana Superdome a deliberate decision—as many believe—to force poorer residents to leave the city?

15. The French Quarter has one of the highest densities of restaurants in the nation. Once the acute shortages of food and water at the Superdome and the Convention Center were known, why didn't officials requisition supplies from hotels and restaurants located just a few blocks away? (As it happened, vast quantities of food were simply left to spoil.)

16. City Hall's emergency command center had to be abandoned early in the crisis because its generator supposedly ran out of diesel fuel. Likewise, many critical-care patients died from heat or equipment failure after hospital backup generators failed. Why were supplies of diesel fuel so inadequate? Why were so many hospital generators located in basements that would obviously flood?

17. Why didn't the Navy or Coast Guard immediately airdrop life preservers and rubber rafts in flooded districts? Why wasn't such life-saving equipment stocked in schools and hospitals?

18. Why weren't evacuee centers established in Audubon Park and other unflooded parts of Uptown, where locals could be employed as cleanup crews?

19. Is the Justice Department investigating the Jim Crow-like response of the suburban Gretna police, who turned back hundreds of desperate New Orleans citizens trying to walk across the Mississippi River Bridge—an image reminiscent of Selma in 1965? New Orleans, meanwhile, abounds in eyewitness accounts of police looting and illegal shootings: Will any of this ever be investigated?

20. Who is responsible for the suspicious fires that have swept the city? Why have so many fires occurred in blue-collar areas that have long been targets of

proposed gentrification, such as the Section 8 homes on Constance Street in the Lower Garden District or the wharfs along the river in Bywater?

21. Where were FEMA's several dozen vaunted urban search-and-rescue teams? Aside from some courageous work by Coast Guard helicopter crews, the early rescue effort was largely mounted by volunteers who towed their own boats into the city after hearing an appeal on television.

22. We found a massive Red Cross presence in Baton Rouge but none in some of the smaller Louisiana towns that have mounted the most impressive relief efforts. The poor Cajun community of Ville Platte, for instance, has at one time or another fed and housed more than 5,000 evacuees; but the Red Cross, along with FEMA, has refused almost daily appeals by local volunteers to send professional personnel and aid. Why then give money to the Red Cross?

23. Why isn't FEMA scrambling to create a central registry of everyone evacuated from the greater New Orleans region? Will evacuees receive absentee ballots and be allowed to vote in the crucial February municipal elections that will partly decide the fate of the city?

24. As politicians talk about "disaster czars" and elite-appointed reconstruction commissions, and as

architects and developers advance utopian designs for an ethnically cleansed "new urbanism" in New Orleans, where is any plan for the substantive participation of the city's ordinary citizens in their own future?

25. Indeed, on the fortieth anniversary of the 1965 Voting Rights Act, what has happened to democracy?

In the Shadow of Disaster

by Ari Kelman

[from the January 2, 2006 issue]

THE FLOOD WAS voracious; it swallowed whole neighborhoods, ending hundreds of lives. But the battered levees have been repaired. They again stand between New Orleans and catastrophe, holding the Mississippi and Lake Pontchartrain in check. The antique drainage system, too, is back online. Any water that falls in the city, every drop of rain or tear shed, ultimately flows through canals until it's pumped over the levee into the lake. This is how New Orleans has been engineered: to control stray water, to clarify the border between the city and its surroundings.

It has been a losing battle. And yet, though it sounds particularly odd following Hurricane Katrina, the city's efforts have been spurred by the notion that nature favors it. From New Orleans' founding near the mouth of the Mississippi in 1718, the city has banked on geography to sweep it to greatness.

IN THE SHADOW OF DISASTER

Long before technologies circumvented the vagaries of geography, boosters claimed the city would reign over a commercial empire. But the local environs rarely cooperated with imperial visions. The lake and river loom above the city. Much of New Orleans lies below sea level, atop a high water table; there's no natural drainage. And pestilence thrives in the steamy delta. Scholars call this the disjuncture between "site"—the actual real estate a city occupies—and "situation"—an urban area's relative advantages as compared with other places. New Orleans, with access to the river and the gulf, enjoys a near-perfect situation. But it has an equally horrid site.

Geographer Peirce Lewis sums it up: New Orleans is "impossible" yet "inevitable." He means that if a city's situation is good enough, people will improve its site—no matter the costs. New Orleanians historically have done this by segregating spaces: at first not socioeconomically or racially but environmentally. In New Orleans there are spaces for nature: outside the levees or within the canals leading from the city. And there are spaces for human endeavors: within town. People here, nature there. The idea is simple, its execution impossible.

For now, water in the city seems under control again, back where people want it: in showers stripping away lingering grime, in strong coffee and confined behind the levees. Still, there's danger. Facing the challenge of rebuilding, New Orleans seems stuck in the mud—not just mired in the muck caking the city but also trapped by centuries of policy mistakes, especially the fantasy that it can be separated from its surroundings. This notion has been as destructive as the worst flood, and as difficult to avoid.

The people charged with rebuilding New Orleans seem

enthralled by this mirage. They serve on committees—Mayor Ray Nagin's and Governor Kathleen Blanco's—with overlapping purviews and dubious authority. But despite their rivalries, the committees agree on at least one point: Levees must be top priority. Scott Cowen, Tulane University's president and part of Nagin's commission, suggests that without better levees other proposals—"world-class public education," improved housing, burnishing the city's "cultural ambience"—will be pointless. Andy Kopplin, executive director of the governor's panel, concurs: "We have to rebuild levees first, so people believe they're safe." To anyone familiar with the city's ecological history, this sounds like a recipe for more disasters.

From the first, New Orleanians augmented the levees. The project accelerated after an 1849 flood soaked the city for months. Federal authorities, alarmed by the inactivity of the nation's busiest port, sponsored two river studies. The first advocated multi-tiered flood control: levees, spillways and "reservoirs," swaths of wetlands acting like sponges. The second, penned by a future head of the Army Corps of Engineers, was more palatable at a time when wetlands were deemed wasteland. So began a policy known as "levees only." By 1900 New Orleans had levees taller than nearby houses. The river and lake had disappeared behind miniature mountains.

Just one problem: They didn't work. The river became more dangerous, and New Orleans less safe. With its water trapped behind levees, the Mississippi rose higher than ever. But you couldn't tell that to New Orleanians. Not even the huge 1927 flood fully changed their minds. That year the city dynamited a levee fifteen miles downstream, lowering the engorged river and destroying Plaquemines and St. Bernard parishes. The city had purchased its safety by sacrificing its poorer neighbors. (This event has fueled rumors in the Ninth Ward, where some residents and evacuees believe the levee fronting their district was destroyed after Katrina to protect wealthier, whiter areas.)

Still, the levees grew after 1927, despite federal inquiries in which conservationists testified that wetlands loss had exacerbated the disaster. The Army Corps of Engineers still refused to add wetlands to its arsenal. Instead, it built New Orleans a spillway that could shunt part of the river into Lake Pontchartrain—and, through the 1950s, continued to raise the levees.

Meanwhile, the city went on a building binge abetted by a drainage system constructed early in the twentieth century. For 200 years New Orleans had been trapped—a long, thin city on a narrow strip of relatively high ground shadowing the river. The Mississippi had flowed on one side, and a cypress wetland, the "backswamp," had stood on the other. After 1900, though, the city began reclaiming wetlands and expanding onto lower ground. By the 1960s the Lakefront neighborhood, the Lower Ninth Ward and other areas had replaced the backswamp. Ecological constraints had again yielded to ambition in a city captivated by its situation. With levees towering and wetlands gone, the segregation of landscapes seemed complete.

Sorting space had two other byproducts. First, more segregation: racial and socioeconomic this time. Before the 1950s New Orleans was a mixed city. Rich, poor, white, nonwhite—all were neighbors. This wasn't by choice but necessity; with development confined to high ground near the river, there wasn't room for people to move into socially segregated enclaves. But when developers started building tract housing on drained land in the city and nearby suburbs, New Orleanians became stratified, with poorer people of color often concentrated on low land and affluent whites typically occupying higher ground, if not the 'burbs.

The second consequence: Controlling nature became harder. Swamps disappeared, both because of urban reclamation and because levees diminished wetlands by keeping floodwaters from recharging the ecosystem. Oil exploration caused coastal erosion and swallowed thousands of acres of wetlands. For every foot the levees grew, it became that much harder to pump water out of the city. Finally, New Orleans began to sink as its watery foundation was replaced by spongy reclaimed land that compacted beneath the city's weight. Urban-environmental feedback loops caused the very problems New Orleanians had been trying to engineer out of their city's site for centuries.

In this setting Katrina made landfall. Its storm surge was too much for the levees. Water overtopped some; others collapsed. The pumps couldn't keep up, and New Orleans filled with water. Mostly the poor, people of color, the infirm and the elderly were left behind. Many died on low ground. The Brookings Institution reports that thirty-eight of greater New Orleans' forty-nine poorest districts flooded. In the city proper, 80 percent of the flooded neighborhoods were majority non-white. Segregation—environmental, socioeconomic and racial—resulted in segregated suffering.

The call now for improved levees is predictable. Joe Canizaro of the mayor's commission worries that nobody will return until they "feel safe." He's right. But what if people feel safe yet aren't? Before Katrina, disaster amnesia and denial allowed people to ignore the danger. Past disasters, says engineer Robert Bea of the University of California, Berkeley, were "alarm bells, but New Orleans kept hitting snooze." The city now has to rethink flood control.

Like most engineers, Bea is certain that levees can be constructed to withstand a Category 5 storm. "It's just a matter of political will and funding," he says. But the funding isn't pocket change; the project requires billions. No one knows where that money will come from. While President Bush has promised the Feds will pay for levee repairs, he hasn't made the same promise about levee improvements. If the money is found, the political will must be sustained across fifteen years, the time needed to build levees to a Category 5 standard.

Even if those levees finally get built, they won't do the trick by themselves; engineers will have to learn to work with the city's peculiar ecology rather than trying to dominate it. "Wetlands must be part of the solution," Bea says. If swamps aren't reintroduced, storm surges will overwhelm even the best levees. And if ocean levels keep rising and New Orleans keeps sinking, the city will drown again.

Craig Colten, a Louisiana State University geographer, agrees. He insists low-lying parts of the city shouldn't be rebuilt. His proposal is extremely controversial, with displaced residents understandably invoking their "right of return" and with most members of the reconstruction committees reluctant to reintegrate wetlands into the city after Mayor Nagin got burned for suggesting that the Ninth Ward might not be rebuilt. But Colten still believes that part of the backswamp should ooze into selected low-lying areas. An equitable method, he believes, would be to "take land from many neighborhoods—Lakefront, Ninth Ward, Gentilly—and relocate rich, poor, middle class to denser settlement on higher ground."

Colten's "new New Orleans," then, would resemble the old New Orleans—from an era before wetlands vanished. It would also touch off battles over whose neighborhoods should be abandoned.

Danielle Taylor, dean of humanities at Dillard University, is certain that the outcome of such fights would favor the powerful. Returning urban districts to swampland, she contends, will shred the urban fabric, wrecking communities that made the city what it was. This echoes the views of Ninth Ward residents, who believe the city's elites saw the flood as the first in what will be waves of urban renewal. Absent affordable housing, redevelopment would leave no room for the poor and people of color, Taylor says. New Orleans would become a sterile—and white—preservation mall, with the French Quarter its anchor store. Colten sympathizes but says that allowing people to return to the lowest land would be "irresponsible."

What's certain is that segregating spaces hasn't worked. As Katrina demonstrated, it's impossible to separate social and environmental issues in this city. New Orleans isn't just a human artifact. Nor, of course, is it wholly natural. It's both: a network of human and nonhuman intermingled, straddling the nature/culture divide. The city must be rebuilt on a more solid foundation: the understanding that allowing no room for nature is as counterproductive as it is unlikely to succeed.

A fresh approach might yield sustainable urban spaces and environmental justice. But this would require hard choices unlikely to be made by committee. Sadly, New Orleans seems destined to find itself where it always has been: in harm's way.

Katrina Lives

by Susan Straight

[from the January 2, 2006 issue]

T HE NATION MIGHT believe it has moved on from
Katrina, from the name so childish and somehow
slightly foreign, not Sherry or Ann or Margaret. Moved on from
the scenes of dark-skinned people in exodus—massed in parking lots with faces upturned as if seeking communion or advice
or comfort from above, wading through iridescent oiled water
up to their thighs, pushing shopping carts, the burros of poor
American neighborhoods, loaded with belongings for the exodus. Sometimes, the soft bodies of children were contorted by
sleep into impossible shapes, wedged in between the boxes or
where a purse would rest if the cart were in a civilized place—
say, a grocery store.

But recently, in a municipal auditorium in Southern California, across the country from Louisiana, in a crowd of
1,700 for a touring black theater production, a comedian

warmed up the audience (maybe ten white or Latino people were present) with Katrina, because black Americans have not finished with her.

He began, "Y'all, Katrina was haaard on us. She beat us down, didn't she?"

The audience began to shout.

"She wasn't no Category 4 hurricane, y'all. She was a Section 8 hurricane, man, from the projects! Look at her name. Katrina! She sound like she Section 8, don't she?"

The audience screamed with laughter.

The comedian's bald head shone and he threw out his arms. "She was whamming around, banging on doors, hollering, 'Is it a man in there? A man?' "

Then he whirled across the stage with arms outstretched, shrieking improvised karate-style calls as the hurricane moved through the landscape the audience saw.

"HE BETTA HAVE my check! I'ma get wild up in here in Louisiana! Where's my money?!"

I'm paraphrasing here, because I was surrounded by clapping and stomping feet and all of our calls, so loud the comedian waited patiently, expertly, for enough quiet to move on.

"Now, the brother with the TV? Where the hell was he going? Where did he plan to plug that sucker in?"

And everyone knew exactly who he was talking about. Everyone in America saw him, right?

But then the comedian shook his head. "Katrina whupped up on us, y'all," he said. "White folks were evacuees. We were refugees. We were looters. White folks were finders."

He waited for the laughter to die.

"No, y'all, for real. But some white folks were cool." He stalked off to the right side of the stage and began to hitch up his pants. "The government was treating us so bad, like dogs, y'all, that even the Klan stepped in." He pulled his pants up higher, moved his shoulders and changed his whole face. "They sure did." He paced the stage deliberately, slowly, and said in a Klan voice, "Man, the government cain't do this to y'all. It ain't constitutional. We can do it, but the government cain't. Even I feel bad for y'all."

He reached behind him and took the white handkerchief he'd been using to wipe sweat from his scalp and draped it over his head and face, and the audience went wilder. He bent slightly and imitated the man reaching out a hand as if from a boat or plane and said, "Come on, Fred, get in. No, get in! I'm tryin' to help ya!" He shook the proffered hand. "Oh, OK—it's me, George, OK?" He lifted up the handkerchief so the audience could see his face again. "Now, get up outta the water and come on."

When the stomping and screams died down, he wiped his face again and smiled. "Anybody out there from New Orleans?"

A group of ten or so, mostly women, hollered and waved from the floor seats.

"You made it, y'all!" he said, and waved back.

Sitting beside me was my girlfriend E, who lived in East New Orleans for five years before coming to California to work in the same office with me. East New Orleans was hit hard; her former home was underwater. Her sister lived in Metairie, and the sister's daughters lived Uptown. All had evacuated to Shreveport, to a motel, the night before Katrina struck. For two months they had been living hand to mouth in two motel rooms, eight people, with no assistance from the Red Cross, FEMA or any other government agency. One daughter's boyfriend worked for Best Buy, and his company had been paying for the motel rooms. None of E's sister's friends or relatives outside Louisiana could send her cash, because she had no bank, no account and nowhere to cash the checks. She also had no post office box or address at the motel. By now, they had no patience.

That night, before the theater production began, E told me her sister had become frustrated and wanted to return to her apartment in Metairie to assess the damage and see if she still had a job at Tulane University, where she'd been working for years. Her daughters all insisted on accompanying her to New Orleans. Their homes were total losses, as were their cars. The Metairie apartment had minimal damage, but now the motel rooms in Shreveport were lost, so all eight people are crowded into a two-bedroom apartment, with no jobs and no money.

"And they never got checks from FEMA?" I asked E.

She raised her eyebrows and said in her wryest voice, "Nope. But Pookie done got his check."

"Huh?" I said. "Pookie?"

She grinned. "You know. Pookie. He lives in Philly, but his girlfriend's cousin's grandma lived in New Orleans last year, and he's got an address, so he got his check from FEMA."

"Oh, no," I said. "You mean Pookie."

"Two thousand dollars," E said, shaking her head. "Mmm, mmm, mmm."

A few weeks later E's sister found out she was laid off from Tulane, as was everyone else she knew, and her last check was the one she got on November 1.

On the other side of me at the theater was our friend T, who works for the IRS. She said, "Don't get me started on the damn government and Katrina. They came into the office last week and told us we can't hire anybody, because we're getting millions cut out of our budget to pay for Katrina. Somebody's getting paid for Katrina, but it damn sure doesn't sound like the people who need it."

I have gotten e-mails from several places in Louisiana where churches and communities are still housing and feeding and clothing hurricane victims, months later, without ever having seen a government official or Red Cross employee. These are small towns where evacuees showed up because they had family nearby, or because geographically this seemed a safe place, or because that's where they ran out of gas. In California I have heard the same stories over and over. No government. No money. Just what we are all giving, as citizens. And Katrina has made hundreds of thousands of African-Americans feel as if they are not, even now, citizens of this country.

Americans, and people around the world, registered shock and disbelief at the images of dark-skinned people, many with foreign-sounding vaguely French accents, fleeing their pastel-painted, oddly ornate old homes after Katrina. Ancient cramped homes filled with people who had no cars and not enough money to leave New Orleans. Many were fifth- or sixth-generation Louisianans. Why had they stayed in this dangerous city, which should not have been built where it was, and why did they have so little?

No one brought up the slave markets or Congo Square. New Orleans and its surrounding areas were the heart of the immense slave trade in America for more than 100 years.

Africans were brought by ship to New Orleans in great numbers, and even after America took the colony from France, made it a state and then banned importation of African slaves, black people were bought and sold in Louisiana through piracy and interstate trade.

In the 1830s, during Alexis de Tocqueville's historic journey through America, he interviewed the French consul of New Orleans, Guillemin, who told him: "New Orleans has a very great future. If we succeed in conquering, or only in greatly diminishing, the scourge of yellow fever, New Orleans is certainly destined to become the largest city in the New World. In fifty years the Mississippi valley will hold the mass of the American population, and here we hold the gate to the river."

The Mississippi Valley held a huge percentage of the nation's wealth before the Civil War, and Louisiana plantations were populated by thousands of slaves. When Katrina hit, many of their descendants fled rising waters and wind, and looked into television cameras with their own incredulity, asking for a ride away from hell. "I am a citizen of the United States," one woman repeated over and over, waiting with her bundles of possessions beside a freeway overpass.

"Katrina," the comedian said ruefully, closing his warm-up act before the theater production began, the people all around me breathing hard with the aftermath of cathartic laughter, some even wiping their cheeks. "She whupped on us, didn't she?"

• • •

Us. PEOPLE NODDED and held up their hands in the darkness of the theater. Citizens of the United States, who are still living in shelters and motels and cars, whose lives will never be the same, not only because water and wind tried to erase those lives but because their lives were negated and minimized and feared and then turned off, on television, after three months.

Even now, as Mayor Ray Nagin begs people to return to New Orleans, residents of the decimated Ninth Ward are being allowed to visit their neighborhood only for a brief time, just to see if anything is salvageable. Houses were moved off foundations, destruction was nearly total and news photos show that in area after area, not even a piece of wood or roof has been moved for cleanup yet.

I met two Louisianans recently who described New Orleans with a kind of shock and awe—they were shocked themselves, and they'd grown up in the swamps. "In the city you can go buy a refrigerator," one said. "But you can't get delivery until January, maybe February. So you'll see some woman toting a hand-cart, pulling a refrigerator over the bridge into the city. Huffing and puffing. Like Mad Max or something."

"This long," the other one said, "and we're just now getting water. Just now."

As layer upon layer of government sifts through requests for funding, Louisianans are beginning to give up.

Years from now, when someone says to a man, "What happened to that '56 Chevy you used to have?" he'll say the one word. When someone says to a teenager, "You were born in New Orleans but you graduated from high school here in Minnesota?" the girl will think the one word.

When someone says, "Your grandfather died in 2005?" there will be the unspoken lament. When someone says to a whole generation of Louisianans, "What happened?" there will be the one-word answer.

Katrina.

In that way, her name will be added to the list that every black American knows, from both handed-down and newly created stories, told by grandparents or children. The names that call up shared knowledge and define moments in hurt and rage—Tuskegee, Tulsa, Rodney King and before him Eula Love, Scottsboro, Jonestown, and MOVE and SLA.

Katrina.

New Orleans Blues

by The Editors

[from the January 2, 2006 issue]

THREE MONTHS AGO, after chafing from criticism over his failure to even appear to respond to the suffering in New Orleans, George W. Bush finally made it to Jackson Square to deliver his promise that "this great city will rise again." Yet today the great city remains largely in darkness. Most citizens of New Orleans are outside its boundaries, many with no real prospect of returning. What's rising in New Orleans are divorce and suicide rates, toxic dumps, foreclosures and rage.

The rage was evident in early December just a half-dozen blocks from Jackson Square, in Congo Square, where African-Americans performed ancestral music in the early nineteenth century, heralding a new American culture. On a recent chilly Saturday, Congo Square was the meeting point for a crowd of about 500 demonstrators who gathered to march behind the

Soul Rebels Brass Band to demand the return of New Orleanians to New Orleans.

By now it should be obvious that the drowning of the city was a man-made disaster. Multiple investigations, including those sponsored by the American Society of Civil Engineers and the National Science Foundation, conclude that the sea walls and levees were poorly designed, constructed and inspected. A not-too-subtle whispering campaign quickly suggested that the fault might lie with those gaudy New Orleanians who insist on rollicking below sea level, or with a state whose legacy of political shenanigans dates back to before "The Kingfish," Huey Long. The city and state have much to account for, including an evacuation plan that failed to protect their most vulnerable citizens. But the ongoing campaign against New Orleans obscures the simple truth that erecting barriers against floods is a federal responsibility. The Army Corps of Engineers failed its job. The Bush Administration now has the obligation to launch a massive effort to rebuild the city that the federal government destroyed.

Bush last visited the Gulf Coast on October 11. It shouldn't surprise anyone that the President, and many in Congress, would prefer to look the other way while New Orleans collapses. Over the past quarter-century, conservatives have waged their most effective war against "big government." This model was advanced by Ronald Reagan and endorsed by every President since. Now, when a federally coordinated solution is required, agencies from HUD to the EPA to FEMA are flummoxed. Bush faithfully followed the script by endorsing only limited solutions like the Gulf Opportunity Zone and Worker Recovery Accounts. In doing so, he advanced government as a stopgap for what couldn't be handled by his private and faith-based "armies of compassion."

Stymied by this lack of leadership and by no national call for an ambitious regional rebuilding effort, Louisiana legislators, among them Democratic Representative William Jefferson and Republican Senator David Vitter, are now fretting aloud that demands for protection from the strongest hurricanes could actually work against the city's interests by raising hopes too high. That's pathetic. A half-day's drive through New Orleans—at least, through the 80 percent of it that still looks nearly exactly as it did three months ago—should reveal to anyone what happens when levees don't hold. You can start by reading the body count still scrawled in red marker on some homes. Yet there are those who dare to offer New Orleans protection on the cheap.

In October this magazine called for a coordinated "people's reconstruction" that would provide for a "democratically accountable, economically viable, socially just and environmentally sustainable plan for regional rebuilding." This effort must begin with the physical reclaiming of New Orleans—an ambitious, two-step process including a re-engineered levee system capable of withstanding a Category 5 hurricane and a fully funded restoration of the coast, using the Coast 2050 blueprint. A people's reconstruction would then address the multiple effects of urban poverty that opened like fresh wounds during those days immediately following the levee breaches. Long before Katrina entered the Gulf, far too many New Orleanians lived on dangerous streets, worked low-paying jobs in the service industry, were unable to insure their families and sent their children to bleak public schools long abandoned by the middle class. For these citizens, the desperation experienced in post-Katrina New Orleans is nothing new.

New Orleans could become the nation's classroom. A reinvigorated dialogue about urban America is newly possible—or at least it was three months ago, when images of suffering children on Louisiana bridges and highways played across the nation's TV screens. So far, the President has squandered this opportunity, just as he squandered the post-9/11 opportunity to realign the nation's energy policy. No wonder it's widely feared in New Orleans that the Katrina moment has passed.

If New Orleans is to reclaim its greatness, the scope of the solution must match the scope of the problem. Each inch of the 200 miles of levees that are supposed to keep the city dry is now suspect. The wetlands that buffer the region continue their relentless disappearing act. Bush's EPA has downplayed the effects of oil spills following the hurricane; there is no real plan to deal with the toxic refuse of the flood. The Administration does not acknowledge the science of global warming and the consequences of a warmer ocean. Many New Orleanians long to return to their homes, but it is an unsteady feeling to raise children and care for elderly parents in a city on the brink. Meanwhile, decisions about homes, neighborhoods, schools and jobs will be made in their absence and without their input.

It doesn't have to be this way. At the beginning of the twentieth century, the rhythms of Congo Square sprouted into jazz, which gave the world a soundtrack of improvisation and democracy. A hundred years later, another democratic revolution could begin in New Orleans—but its song is quickly playing out.

Hard Times
in the Big Easy

by Gary Younge

[from the March 13, 2006 issue]

" JUST AS THE Carthaginians hired mercenaries to
do their fighting for them, we Americans bring in
mercenaries to do our hard and humble work," wrote John
Steinbeck in *Travels with Charley*. "I hope we may not be overwhelmed one day by peoples not too proud or too lazy or too
soft to bend to the earth and pick up the things we eat."

Almost fifty years later the economy still cannot function
without migrant labor. "Because natural population increase is
unlikely to provide sufficient workers, immigration will play
a critical role in sustaining the labor force growth needed to
maintain overall economic growth," the Immigration Policy
Center concluded in November.

The paradox is that the country's political culture cannot
function without scapegoating migrant laborers either. In
December the House passed the Sensenbrenner bill, one of the
most draconian pieces of anti-immigrant legislation in a

generation. Meanwhile the vigilante Minutemen, no longer content to "patrol" the borders looking for illegal immigrants to "arrest," have taken to chasing day laborers at pickup sites, shouting, "This is America, not Mexico!" Every weeknight CNN airs xenophobic diatribes from Lou Dobbs posing as the friend of the common people.

No wonder two-thirds of Americans think illegal immigration is "very" or "extremely" serious and three-quarters believe not enough is being done to protect the nation's borders, according to a *Time* poll. Americans, it seems, love immigration. It's just immigrants they can't stand. The principle is central to the mythologies of personal reinvention, social meritocracy, ethnic diversity and class fluidity that lie at the core of the American dream. But the people themselves are often regarded as anathema to it.

THIS IS NOT new. During the mid-1800s Irish Catholics met severe discrimination. Then there was the Chinese Exclusion Act in 1882, and during World War II, Japanese internment. Since 9/11 Muslims have been victimized for security reasons. And for the economy, there are Hispanics. So we are left despising the very people on whom we depend, and immigrants are left with the worst of all worlds—economically marginalized and socially demonized. Vulnerable to unscrupulous employers, opportunistic politicians and racist hatemongers, they work simply to exist in a place where their very existence has become an affront.

Welcome to New Orleans. For this is precisely the contradiction currently unfolding in the rebuilding of the Crescent City. Since Hurricane Katrina the city's Hispanic population has ballooned from 3 percent to an estimated 30 percent. Every morning at Lee Circle hundreds of day laborers gather under the watchful eye of the Confederate general and wait for work. Every night hundreds sleep in a tent city in City Park, Scout Island, where one standpipe and three toilets serve about 200 people.

Globalization brought them here. A system in which one person's overtime is another family's weekly wage will push from despair as much as pull from hope. "You can have a lot of love for your children, but it cannot fill their stomachs," says Mercedes Sanchez, standing outside her tarpaulin home in the tent city. "In Mexico I made 200 pesos a week. I can make that in two hours here." But while capital can roam free, the movement of laborers is restricted and therefore perilous. Sanchez paid $3,000 to trek three days and nights through the Arizona desert. Along the way she was stripped naked by bandits and robbed at gunpoint. "When you walk through the desert, you think you're never going to arrive," she says. "It costs a lot of money and a lot of tears."

Katrina's winds had barely stopped howling before the mood music that created this situation could be heard: George W. Bush suspended the Davis-Bacon Act, which requires employers with government contracts to pay "prevailing" wages, and waived the requirement for contractors to provide I-9 employment eligibility forms completed by their workers. By the time those measures had been restored, their suspension had already signaled a desire to cut corners and pay below-market rates—the ideal conditions for taking on undocumented workers.

Meanwhile, in an address to business owners and contractors, New Orleans Mayor Ray Nagin said he knew what they were thinking: "How do I insure that New Orleans is not overrun by Mexican workers?" His taste for rebuilding a Chocolate City is now renowned; his refusal to stomach one that consists of a sizable portion of crème caramel is only now becoming apparent.

Nagin's words were crude, but his actions have been consistent with a mindset in which Hispanic migrant workers are both crucial and criminalized, encouraged and exploited, accepted and abused. The Southern Poverty Law Center has filed two collective-action lawsuits against two corporations on behalf of up to 2,000 mostly immigrant workers in New Orleans who say they have not been paid or have been underpaid. One is against Belfor USA group. Its attorney, David Kurtz, said, "The allegations are groundless," but refused further comment. The other is against LVI Environmental Services and D&L Environmental Inc., a subcontractor. LVI did not return calls; D&L declined to comment.

Carla (not her real name) worked for D&L pulling down drywall in hospitals, clinics and schools. Starting November 9 she was promised $12 an hour and $18 for overtime and worked from 7 A.M. until 5 P.M. seven days a week. By Thanksgiving she still had not received a cent. When she went to pick up her check, she claims, her boss told her it hadn't been issued because of a computer error. When she started to cry and demand the money security guards threatened her with forcible removal.

There is a name for a system in which you make people work and don't pay them. It's called slavery. It's the institution that built this beautiful city, and its legacy was laid bare by Katrina last year. At that time, as thousands converged on the convention center, then-FEMA director Michael Brown said, "We're seeing people that we didn't know exist." Once again, it seems, the presence of those having hard times in the Big Easy has conveniently escaped the authorities' attention, even as their pain is hidden in plain sight.

Bush's New Storm

by Michael Tisserand

[from the March 6, 2006 issue]

NEARLY HALF A year after federally built levees crumpled around New Orleans, the Bush Administration is facing a new storm of its own making. In recent weeks it has proved itself as incapable of managing the Congressional inquiries into its post-Katrina actions as it was of managing the hurricane response itself. But there's one difference: In this new storm, at least, one gets the impression that Team Bush is doing its very best.

Here's one way you can tell they're trying: Minnesota Senator Norm Coleman is on message. If you want to discern the White House's talking points, it always pays to check out Coleman, and the Katrina hearings are no exception. On February 10 Coleman dutifully sprayed verbal buckshot at both Louisiana Governor Kathleen Blanco and New Orleans Mayor Ray Nagin, before narrowing in on the day's star witness: former Federal

Emergency Management Agency head Michael Brown. And so two political hacks—one elected, one appointed—turned on each other. Coleman entreated Brown to "put a mirror in front of your face" and "confess your own sins." But Brown, perhaps realizing that his designated role as fall guy won't give him much of a boost in his new private-sector career—disaster consulting—refused to play along.

Brown has no defense. He had advanced his appearance before the committee by telling the *New York Times* that the "real story" is the faulty structure of FEMA, a once-sturdy agency that collapsed when George W. Bush folded it into Homeland Security in 2003. The Administration capped its restructuring by naming inexperienced pals to top positions, with Brown as Exhibit A (Brown skipped this point in his testimony). At the time, Brown crowed that his agency was "FEMA on steroids," as first reported by Jon Elliston in a 2004 investigation. Now, in front of the committee, Brown blamed the "disconnect" between FEMA and the Department of Homeland Security for the agency's inability to function when faced with an actual emergency.

But Coleman refused to give up. "You didn't provide the leadership," he assailed. "Even with structural infirmities, strong leadership can overcome that. And clearly that wasn't the case here." Coleman got that one right, albeit unintentionally. The destruction of New Orleans and the still-climbing official death toll, which now stands at more than 1,300, is the direct consequence of weak leadership from the top—the White House. The flawed federal levee system and the botched response resulted in this country's most deadly man-made disaster. The waters have long since receded, but, despite occasional vague murmurs of affection from Bush, New Orleans is still struggling to function as a modern American city. Nobody's confessing anything here. The travesty deserves an independent investigation and full participation from the White House. Instead, it received Republican-led inquiries and no direct access to the President.

Yet even the compromised investigation is unearthing startling facts about how this country responds to an urban catastrophe. In testimony and in details emerging from hundreds of thousands of documents, the scenes are of an Administration and its agencies that, when disaster strikes, stumble over one another in ways that would be high slapstick, if only it were a movie. E-mails, phone calls and even eyewitness accounts alerted the White House as early as Monday, August 29, that people were stranded and waters were rising—but it didn't deter Homeland Security Secretary Michael Chertoff from flying to Atlanta to hash over the threat of avian flu, or Bush from flying to the side of country singer Mark Willis to get his picture taken while hashing out some guitar vamps. Words like "disconnected" and "disengaged" dominate the Congressional findings. This disconnect preceded the storm, when the nation's response plan wasn't followed. It occurred during the storm and in its aftermath, when New Orleans citizens clutched starving babies and screamed at CNN cameras. And it continues to this day.

For New Orleanians, Bush delivered a clear sign that he remains disengaged when he nixed—without offering a viable alternative—the Baker bill, an ambitious plan to purchase and restore ruined homes, and then faulted Louisiana for not coming up with a plan. Then there was the State of the Union address, devoid of even a moment of silence for the men, women and children who died on the streets and in their attics. The only mention of what happened in New Orleans came in four sentences toward the speech's end—in a segment about compassion. It's not about compassion. It's about justice. Americans must realize that we are all responsible for rebuilding New Orleans and funding Category 5 hurricane protection, including coastal restoration. This will require a national effort, led by the president. But so far, this president doesn't appear to be up to the job. "One thing that I have found is a strong correlation between effective leadership and effective response," said Republican Senate homeland security committee chair Susan Collins with candor. "Unfortunately, I have also found the converse to be true." House investigators were even more direct, stating that "earlier presidential involvement might have resulted in a more effective response."

Details are still emerging from the inquiries. But we already know enough to know that we need an independent investigation; that Chertoff, the president's top adviser on national disasters, should immediately be relieved of his duties; and that Bush and Dick Cheney should be compelled to testify. As New Orleans labors to rebuild its hospitals, its courts, its neighborhoods, its cultural life, its schools, its streets, its businesses, its homes, its public transportation, its police force, its environment and everything else that makes a city a city, it deserves restitution. A half-year after the storm, not one New Orleanian should be without a home because of a president who failed to protect a city and hesitated to save its citizens.

Neglect in New Orleans

by The Editors

[from the April 10, 2006 issue]

MORE THAN SIX months after one of the worst natural disasters to hit the United States, a perfect storm of malign neglect on the federal, state and local levels continues to batter the victims of Hurricane Katrina. The overwhelming scale of destruction wrought by the hurricane required a comprehensive, federally directed plan of reconstruction, including the rebuilding of levees and the restoration of coastal wetlands, yet the record of the past six months is one of promises unkept, funding delayed and denied, and machinations of politicians and their corporate cronies to profit from the catastrophe. The net effect has been the disenfranchisement and continued displacement of the poor and minority population of New Orleans, which suffered disproportionately from the hurricane.

After months of delay, in late March the House approved a

$19.1 billion Gulf Coast aid package, including $4.2 billion in block grants for housing needs. Yet as Chris Kromm of Gulf Coast Reconstruction Watch (www.reconstructionwatch.org) points out, the bill—passed less than three months before June 1, the official start of hurricane season—comes way too late and is far short of what's needed. The House rejected an amendment that would have provided $465 million to strengthen levees. And although the bill includes $1 billion to rebuild rental housing—crucial, since most displaced residents were renters— Congress turned back an amendment that would have prevented FEMA from evicting residents from temporary housing until alternatives were found (even as the bill was passed, families were being evicted from hotels in New Orleans).

The House bill does little or nothing to fix other structural problems, including the city's devastated healthcare system (fifteen out of the city's twenty-two hospitals are now closed, including Charity Hospital, which cared for most of the city's uninsured population), its public school system (only twenty of 117 pre-storm schools are functioning, sixteen of them now as charter schools) and its toxin-laden environment. And the Senate doesn't plan to discuss its version of the bill until May.

At the same time, the city's black and overwhelmingly Democratic electorate has been effectively disenfranchised. The House rejected an amendment that would have provided $50 million to help storm-ravaged communities organize elections, and the Justice Department approved the first New Orleans municipal elections since the storm, even though the city has no plans to provide out-of-state balloting. Up to two-thirds of the displaced are living out of state, a large majority African-American.

The neglect at the federal level is matched by the hijacking of democratic structures at the local level. As Mike Davis demonstrates in his article, "Who is Killing New Orleans?" (*The Nation*, April 10, 2006), the city's reconstruction effort has been taken over by a coterie of business elites and real estate developers, who have used mayor-appointed commissions to bypass elected officials in an effort to turn New Orleans into a smaller, whiter, more conservative city.

But the people of New Orleans are fighting back. The community-organizing group ACORN and other grassroots organizations, including the People's Hurricane Relief Fund, the Common Ground collective, the Justice Center and the New Orleans Green Party, are working to repair homes, rebuild communities and fight for the rights of displaced citizens. They've been joined recently by military veterans who make the connection between the destruction of Iraq and the devastation of New Orleans. One Iraq War vet is quoted on *The Nation*'s website as saying, "What my country has become sickens me." The people of New Orleans need his solidarity—and ours—if the city's second Reconstruction is to avoid going the way of the first.

Suppressing the N.O. Vote

by The Editors

[from the May 1, 2006 issue]

NEW ORLEANS HAS long been pivotal in the strug-gle for black voting rights. During the Civil War, free blacks there demanded suffrage; their efforts resulted in Lincoln's first public call for voting rights for some blacks in the final speech of his life. Once these rights were won, New Orleans's blacks took an active part in politics, leading to the establishment of the South's only integrated public school system. But rights once gained aren't necessarily secure; after Reconstruction, blacks in New Orleans lost the right to vote. As Thomas Wentworth Higginson wrote at the time of the Civil War, "revolutions may go backwards."

This is what we are seeing now, as New Orleans prepares for municipal elections on April 22. These elections are set to take place even though fewer than half the city's 460,000 residents have returned and the vast majority of those displaced outside Louisiana are African-Americans—the result of what Representative Barney Frank calls the Bush Administration's policy of "ethnic cleansing by inaction."

How did this happen? How did New Orleans become the most obvious symbol of the "backwards revolution" in voting rights that's been going on for at least twenty-five years? The answer is a states' rights mentality that pervades not just the Louisiana legislature but also the Bush Administration. As the Rev. Jesse Jackson wrote recently, the Administration "seems intent on suppressing the African-American vote in New Orleans and in Louisiana."

Starting months ago, civil rights advocates raised concerns about trying to hold an election in New Orleans with so many black residents spread all over the country, most in temporary, often shifting housing and likely to have a hard time finding out who's running, let alone getting and returning absentee ballots. Let evacuees cast their votes in major centers of the diaspora, the advocates urged, much as Mexicans and Iraqis living in the United States have participated in their home country elections by voting at satellite stations.

But Louisiana rejected that idea out of hand; instead, the state legislature approved a proposal that allowed absentee ballots and limited in-state satellite voting and got it approved by the Justice Department (which under the Voting Rights Act of 1965 must clear changes in voting procedures that could discriminate against black voters or reduce black electoral strength). Justice officials went so far as to claim that "minority members of the Louisiana House and Senate were unanimous" in supporting the plan, a claim roundly disputed by elected black leaders, including State Senator Cleo Fields.

Despite such overtly discriminatory actions, Democratic Party leaders have offered only listless support of voting rights efforts—Democratic National Committee chair Howard Dean called the Justice Department decision "a disappointing development." There have even been rumors that some Democrats in Washington welcome the dispersal of the African-American voters of New Orleans as a way of building up party strength elsewhere. Reverend Jackson, in recent remarks at the *Nation* office, said "Democrats are soft-shoeing" on the voting rights issue. Joining him in the New Orleans fight have been the NAACP, ACORN and the Congressional Black Caucus, most notably John Conyers.

The Supreme Court declared more than a century ago that the equal right to vote is fundamental because it is "preservative of all rights." The New Orleans election will not only determine who will lead the city but also play a major role in deciding how the city's schools will be reconstituted, who will get to live where and whether reconstruction contracts and jobs will be fairly distributed. Every citizen of New Orleans has the right to participate in those decisions. But thanks to a hostile Administration and an indifferent opposition, that will not happen.

The Battle of New Orleans

by Gary Younge

[from the May 8, 2006 issue]

"THERE ARE TWO types of power," said Linda Jeffers, addressing an accountability session of New Orleans mayoral candidates at the city's Trinity Episcopal Church. "Organized money and organized people." Since Hurricane Katrina the battle between those two forces has shaped the struggle to rebuild New Orleans. Now it is set to intensify.

The one thing both seem to agree on is that neither wants the city to return to the way it was before the hurricane. The people of New Orleans, most of whom are black and many of whom are poor, want schools that will educate their children, jobs that will pay a living wage and neighborhoods where capital investment matches the large pools of social capital created by their churches and close-knit communities. Organized money has something else in mind: the destruction of many of those communities, the permanent removal of those who lived in them and a city that follows the gentrification patterns of racial removal and class cleansing that have played out elsewhere in America. Under these circumstances, the organization of people has been impressive. Grassroots groups have done a remarkable job of cohering those scattered throughout the country into a political constituency.

As Jeffers spoke, the city's mayoral candidates sat before an audience of more than 500 who had been bused in from Tennessee and elsewhere in Louisiana, as well as several hundred evacuees in Houston, Austin, San Antonio and Dallas who were watching the candidates being questioned on satellite. Five days later Jeffers, a leader with the nonprofit Industrial Areas Foundation (IAF), who moved from Gentilly to Houston after Katrina, schlepped through the unforgiving Texas heat distributing food and signing up eighty evacuees for their absentee ballots at the Encore housing complex. Meanwhile, various organizations have been ferrying people from neighboring states to satellite polling stations dotted around Louisiana for early voting in the April 22 election.

But they are operating under intolerable conditions, not least where these elections are concerned. By almost any standard—international or local—these elections are neither free nor fair. More than half the city's residents have not returned. But requests for polling stations to be set up in the major towns outside the state where they have resettled were rejected by a federal court judge, a decision supported by the Louisiana legislature. "You're telling me they can do it in Iraq but they can't do it here?" asks Walter Milton, another IAF leader.

As a result, people have to travel hundreds of miles to vote or organize an absentee vote. The overwhelming majority of those who will be most adversely affected are once again black and poor. So Jim Crow is on the ballot. But this is the New South with a new, more subtle but no less effective racism. Black demands for full citizenship no longer fall afoul of the law of the land but instead the law of probability. They were more likely to be flooded, more likely to be displaced, least likely to be able to return and therefore least likely to be able to vote.

With organized people thus thwarted, organized money has asserted itself with great effect. The current mayor, Ray Nagin, was the candidate of big business. Nicknamed Ray Reagan, he came to power in 2002 with a minority of black support and the overwhelming backing of whites and the business community. But then, in November [2000], he rejected a plan by the Urban Land Institute. The institute had presented a map with three "investment zones." The zones earmarked for mass buyouts and future green zones, and the last to be invested in, were overwhelmingly black: eastern New Orleans and Gentilly; the northern part of Lakeview; and parts of the Lower Ninth Ward, Broadmoor, Mid-City and Hollygrove. New Orleans needed a smaller footprint, they said; but it would be big enough to kick out most African-Americans and the poor.

When Nagin balked, business looked for some viable new candidates. Its favored son this time around is Ron Forman, head of the Audubon Nature Institute. But as a backup, business interests are also investing in the local political aristocracy in the guise of Mitch Landrieu. Landrieu, currently Louisiana's lieutenant governor, is also the brother of Mary Landrieu—one of Louisiana's U.S. senators—and the son of Moon Landrieu, New Orleans's last white mayor, who left office in 1978. So the people have a vote; but business has picked the incumbent and the two main challengers. Unlike Nagin, Landrieu and Forman are white. With little to choose from on substantive issues among the three of them, the voters may base their decision on the symbolism of race. Given everything that happened following Katrina, this is probably inevitable; given the needs of the city as a result, it is regrettable. It will take more than melanin to rebuild this city; indeed, it was an obsession with melanin that destroyed it.

Like teenagers discovering sex, the media developed an intense fascination with the mundane facts of American life following the hurricane: namely, the glaring disparities in race and class that persist and pervade. Having gorged themselves on the undeniable evidence of glaring disparities in race and class, they soon got sick of the subject and went to sleep.

Up in the mostly white and wealthy Garden District, a delicious choice of croissants is offered at the Boulangerie on Magazine Street—mockingly referred to as the "aisle of denial." Down in the Ninth Ward they're still finding dead bodies, nine in March plus a skull, some skeletonized and others half eaten by animals.

One waits in vain for CNN's Anderson Cooper to revive the indignation that elevated him to prime time. But there is no dramatic backdrop to the systematic and systemic exclusions of African-Americans this time around. It's as though corpses have to be floating down the street and thousands stranded without food or water before racism is once more worthy of note. "I came down off my rooftop and I walked through the waters," said Jeffers. "And now I feel like they're taking me back on to the rooftop again." Organized people are trying to move to higher ground; organized money is trying to sell the land beneath their feet.

Contributors

Eric Alterman is Professor of English at Brooklyn College of the City University of New York, media columnist for *The Nation*, the "Altercation" weblogger for MSNBC.com, and a senior fellow at the Center for American Progress, where he writes and edits the "Think Again" column. Alterman is the author of the national bestseller *What Liberal Media?: The Truth About Bias and the News* (Basic Books, 2003). His most recent book is *When Presidents Lie: A History of Deception and Its Consequences* (Viking, 2004). His *Sound & Fury: The Making of the Punditocracy* (Harper Perennial, 1992; Cornell University Press, 2000) won the 1992 George Orwell Award.

Max Blumenthal is a Nation Institute Puffin Foundation writing fellow. His work has appeared in *The Nation, Salon, The American Prospect,* and *The Washington Monthly*. He is a research fellow for Media Matters for America.

Alexander Cockburn has written the "Beat the Devil" column for *The Nation* since 1984. In 1987 he published a collection of essays, *Corruptions of Empire*, and two years later he co-wrote, with Susanna Hecht, *The Fate of the Forest: Developers, Destroyers, and Defenders of the Amazon* (both Verso). Another collection, *The Golden Age Is In Us*, was published in 1995 by Verso. Cockburn also co-edits the newsletter *CounterPunch* with Jeffrey St. Clair. They have recently coauthored several books, including *Imperial Crusades: Iraq, Afghanistan, and Yugoslavia* (Verso, 2004) and *Dime's Worth of Difference: Beyond the Lesser of Two Evils* (AK Press).

Mike Davis is the author of many books, including *City of Quartz* (Verso, 1990), *The Monster at Our Door: The Global Threat of Avian Flu* (The New Press, 2005), and *Planet of Slums* (Verso).

Jon Elliston, news editor for the Asheville, North Carolina, *Mountain Xpress*, is the author of *Disaster in the Making*, an investigative report on FEMA funded by the Association of Alternative Newsweeklies.

Tom Engelhardt, who created and runs The Nation Institute's Tomdispatch.com ("a regular antidote to the mainstream media"), is also Consulting Editor at Metropolitan Books, the co-founder of the American Empire Project, and the author of *The End of Victory Culture*, a history of American triumphalism in the Cold War, as well as the novel *The Last Days of Publishing* (both from University of Massachusetts Press). He is a Fellow of The Nation Institute.

Eric Foner, a member of *The Nation's* editorial board, is the DeWitt Clinton Professor of History at Columbia University. His publications include *Free Soil, Free Labor, Free Men: The Ideology of the Republican Party Before the Civil War* (Oxford University Press, 1970), *The Story of American Freedom* (W.W. Norton & Co., 1998), and *Forever Free: The Story of Emancipation and Reconstruction* (Knopf, 2005). In 2000, he served as President of the American Historical Association.

Anthony Fontenot, a New Orleans native, is pursuing a PhD in architecture at Princeton. He has written on contemporary conditions in Berlin, Beirut, Kabul, and New Orleans.

William Greider, the national affairs correspondent for *The Nation*, is the author of the national bestsellers *One World, Ready or Not; Secrets of the Temple,* and *Who Will Tell the People* (Simon & Schuster, 1998). Greider's latest book is *The Soul of Capitalism: Opening Paths to a Moral Economy* (Simon & Schuster, 2003).

Mark Hertsgaard is a San Francisco–based independent journalist and author. He currently writes as the environment correspondent for *The Nation*, and is the political correspondent for US satellite broadcaster LinkTV. His most recent book is *The Eagle's Shadow: Why America Fascinates and Infuriates the World* (Farrar, Straus and Giroux, 2002).

Katrina vanden Heuvel has been *The Nation*'s editor since 1995. She is the co-editor of *Taking Back America—And Taking Down the Radical Right* (Nation Books, 2004). She is also co-editor (with Stephen F. Cohen) of *Voices of Glasnost: Interviews with Gorbachev's Reformers* (Norton, 1989) and editor of *The Nation: 1865–1990* and the collection *A Just Response: The Nation on Terrorism, Democracy and September 11, 2001*. She is a frequent commentator on American and international politics on MSNBC, CNN, and PBS.

Nicholas von Hoffman is the author of *A Devil's Dictionary of Business*, recently published by Nation Books. He is the author of thirteen books, including *Citizen Cohn* (Bantam, 1998), and is a columnist for the *New York Observer*.

Earl Ofari Hutchinson, a political analyst and social issues commentator, is the author of *The Crisis in Black and Black* (Middle Passage Press, 1998).

Ari Kelman, author of *A River and Its City: The Nature of Landscape in New Orleans*, teaches history at the University of California, Davis.

Michael T. Klare is the defense correspondent of *The Nation* and a professor of peace and world security studies at Hampshire College. His latest book is *Blood and Oil: The Dangers and Consequences of America's Growing Dependence on Imported Petroleum* (Metropolitan Books, 2004).

Naomi Klein is an award-winning journalist and author of the international best-seller *No Logo: Taking Aim at the Brand Bullies*. Translated into twenty-five languages, *No Logo* was called by the *New York Times* "a movement bible." She writes an internationally syndicated column for *The Nation*. A collection of her work, titled *Fences and Windows: Dispatches from the Front Lines of the Globalization Debate*, was published by Picador in October 2002. Her new book is called *Blank is Beautiful: The Rise of Disaster Capitalism*.

Christian Parenti is a correspondent for *The Nation* and is author of *The Freedom: Shadows and Hallucinations in Occupied Iraq* (The New Press, 2004). He received a PhD in sociology from the London School of Economics in 2000. His two previous books are *The Soft Cage: Surveillance in America from Slavery to the War on Terror* (Basic Books, 2003) and *Lockdown America: Police and Prisons in the Age of Crisis* (Verso, 2000). He has been a Soros Senior Justice fellow and a Ford Foundation Fellow at the CUNY Graduate School's Center for Place, Culture, and Politics.

Adolph Reed, Jr., an expatriate New Orleanian, is professor of political science at the University of Pennsylvania and a member of the interim national council of the Labor Party.

Jeremy Scahill, a Puffin writing fellow at The Nation Institute and correspondent for *Democracy Now!*, is an award-winning journalist who has reported extensively from Iraq, Yugoslavia, and the front lines of many social-justice struggles in the United States. He is working on a new book, *Blackwater*, to be published by Nation Books in 2007.

Robert Scheer's columns appear in newspapers across the country. In 1993 he launched a nationally syndicated column based at the *Los Angeles Times*, where he was named a contributing editor. That column ran weekly for the next twelve years and is now based at the *San Francisco Chronicle*. Scheer can be heard on the political radio program *Left, Right and Center* on KCRW, the National Public Radio affiliate in Santa Monica, California. He has written six books. Most recently he co-authored, with his son Christopher and Lakshmi Chaudhry, *The Five Biggest Lies Bush Told Us about Iraq* (Seven Stories Press, 2003).

Billy Sothern, an anti-death-penalty lawyer and writer living in New Orleans, is working on the forthcoming *Down in New Orleans*, a book about the realities of American poverty and racism revealed by Hurricane Katrina, to be published by University of California Press.

Susan Straight's is the author of the novels *Highwire Moon* (Anchor, 2002) and *A Million Nightingales* (Pantheon, 2006).

Michael Tisserand, the former editor of *Gambit Weekly* in New Orleans, is currently working on the book *Sugarcane Academy*, forthcoming from Harcourt.

Nick Turse is the Associate Editor and Research Director of TomDispatch.com. He has written for the *Los Angeles Times*, the *San Francisco Chronicle*, *The Nation*, *The Village Voice*, *Daily Ireland*, and he writes regularly for Tomdispatch.com.

Curtis Wilkie, author of *Dixie: A Personal Odyssey Through Events That Shaped the Modern South* (Scribner, 2001), lives in New Orleans and Oxford, Mississippi, where he holds the Cook Chair in Journalism at the University of Mississippi.

Patricia J. Williams, a professor of law at Columbia University, writes the "Diary of a Mad Law Professor" column for *The Nation*. Her publications include *The Alchemy of Race & Rights* and *The Rooster's Egg* (Harvard University Press; 1993 and 1995, respectively), and, most recently, *Open House: On Family Food, Friends, Piano Lessons, and the Search for a Room of My Own* (Farrar, Straus and Giroux, 2004.)

Gary Younge, the Alfred Knobler Journalism Fellow at The Nation Institute, is the New York correspondent for the *Guardian* and the author of *No Place Like Home: A Black Briton's Journey Through the Deep South* (University Press of Mississippi, 2002) and *Stranger in a Strange Land: Travels in the Disunited States* (New Press, 2006).

Index

A

ACORN, 134–35, 137, 217,
   221
African Americans
   demographics, 60, 130, 167
   politics, 37, 130, 219–21
   poverty, 23–25, 29
   slavery, 199–200
   See also racism
Alexander Strategy Group, 79
Algiers, 61
Allbaugh, Joe, 12, 101, 103–4
American Security Group, 75
Anderson, Sherwood, 39
ANWR (Arctic National
   Wildlife Refuge), 91
Ashcroft, John, 85
Astrodome, 159–60
Audubon, 61, 63

B

Barbour, Haley, 102
Barnes, Fred, 52
Barrios, Renee, 136–37
Baton Rouge, Louisiana, 38
Bauer, Gary, 78
Bea, Robert, 191–92
Bechtel Corporation, 98, 160
Belfor USA, 210
Bell, Reginald, 8
Bernard, Gladys, 133–34
Birmingham, Alabama, 33
Black, Cofer, 79
Black Men of Labor, 139–41
Blackhawk, 75
Blackwater USA, 73–79, 106,
   156
Blanco, Kathleen, 24, 136–37,
   189, 211
Bloomberg, Mayor, 6
Blotner, Joseph, 38
Boeckmann, Alan, 100

Boone, Wellington, 85–86
Bourbon Street, 39
bread and roses, 34
Breaux, Paul, 14–15
Bremer, L.Paul, 74, 97, 99
Bright, Dan, 110
Broussard, Aaron, 11
Brown, Michael, 12, 51–52, 81, 102, 208, 210
Bush, Barbara, 44, 148
Bush, George, Sr., 44
Bush, George W., 139, 206, 214
  and African Americans, 29
  FEMA, 12
  policies, 53–56, 106, 173–75, 205
  and poverty, 24
  press conference, 3, 165
Butler, Benjamin, 36

C
Cafferty, Jack, 52
Cajun cuisine, 40
Cancer Alley, 18
Canizaro, Joe, 191
Card, Robert G., 105
Cavuto, Neil, 52
CH2M Hill, 98
Chaco Canyon, 41
Charity Hospital, 63
Chávez, Hugo, 82
Cheney, Dick, 43, 97, 168, 214

Chertoff, Michael, 3–4, 180, 213–14
Chocolate City, 209
Chopin, Kate, 39
Civil War, 36, 42, 219
Claiborne Avenue, 145
Clapp, Phil, 20
Clinton, Bill, 37
CNN, 51
Coalition on Revival, 85–86
Cole, Tom, 68
Coleman, Norm, 211–12
Collins, Susan, 214
Colson, Charles, 83
Colten, Craig, 190
Common Ground collective, 217
Community Labor United, 149
Comus, 43
Congressional Black Caucus, 221
Connor, Bull, 33
Conyers, John, 174, 221
Cooper, Anderson, 226
CPA (Coalition Provisional Authority), 97
Creole cuisine, 40
Crespo, Daniela, 106

D
D&L Environmental Inc., 210
Daniel, Jamal, 103
Davis-Bacon wage laws, 64, 67, 209

dead zone, 18
Dean, Howard, 221
DeLay, Tom, 50–51, 78
Democracy Now!, 106
Democrats, 28, 162–63, 166, 174–75
DeParle, Jason, 49
Depression, 37
DeVos, Dick, 78
DeVos, Richard, 78
DHS (Department of Homeland Security), 12, 55, 82, 106, 212
Diamond, 18
Dobbs, Lou, 208
Dorsey, Lee, 144
Drennen, Mark, 60–61
Duke, Anne, 74
Duke, David, 37
DynCorp, 75

E

Earley, Mark, 83–84
Edwards, Edwin, 37
Edwards, John, 163
The End of Nature, 19
The End of Victory Culture, 107
Engelhardt, Tom, 95, 107
English, Phil, 68
evacuation, 14, 155
Evangeline Parish, 119–21

F

Faulkner, William, 38–39
Feeney, Tom, 67
Feingold, Russ, 174
FEMA (Federal Emergency Management Agency), 11–15, 55, 81–82, 101, 184, 212
Fields, Barbara, 29
Fields, Cleo, 220
Flaherty, Jordan, 149
Flake, Jeff, 67
Flavin, Christopher, 18
flooding, 49–52, 187
Fluor Corporation, 99
Fontenot, Dolores, 119–21
Fontenot, Edna, 124
Ford, Richard, 39
Forman, Ron, 225–26
Fox, 52
Frank, Barney, 220
French Quarter, 38–39, 61

G

Garden District, 61, 63
Garvey, Meg, 114
Gelbspan, Ross, 19–20
Gingrich, Newt, 162
global warming, 17–21
globalization, 95–96
Green Cross, 8
Green Party, 217
Green Zone, 97
Greenbaum, Tilden, 113–14
Griffith, Lanny, 102–3

Guidry, Danny, 126–28
Gulf Coast Reconstruction
    Watch, 216
Gulf Opportunity Zone, 204

H

Haley, Archie, 8
Halliburton, 104, 160, 168
Harriman, Ed, 99
Harris, Tanya, 133–35, 137
Hastert, Dennis, 4, 44
Haygood, Wil, 49
Haywood, Bill, 34
Hazard Mitigation Grant
    Program, 13
The Heat Is On, 19–20
Hellman, Lillian, 39
Higginson, Thomas
    Wentworth, 217
Hispanic population, 206–7
Holt, David, 65
Holt, Lester, 50
Horan, Bill, 86
Hot 8, 140–41, 145
housing, 61–63, 71–72
Houston, 159–60
Howell, Mike, 9, 14, 154
Hsu, Spencer S., 101
Hume, Brit, 52
Hurricane Andrew, 11
Hurricane Floyd, 13

I

IAF (Industrial Areas
    Foundation), 171–72, 224
immigration, 207–9
Intercon, 75
Iraq, 95–107
ISI (Instinctive Shooting Interna-
    tional), 75, 77

J

Jackson, Alphonso, 130
Jackson, Gary, 79
Jackson, Jesse, 85, 220–21
Jackson, Maynard, 37
jail, 109–16
Jeffers, Linda, 221–22, 226
Jefferson Parish, 13, 37, 61
Jefferson, William, 205
Jeske, Clint, 14
Johnson, Fred, 141
Jones, Rachel, 111–12
Justice Center, 217

K

K-Doe, Antoinette, 144
KBR (Kellogg, Brown & Root),
    97–98
Keating, Frank, 104
Kennedy, Edward, 163, 169
Knocke, Russ, 77
Krasnoff, Mark, 126, 129–31
Krauthammer, Charles, 52

Krewe of Barkus, 39
Kromm, Chris, 216
Krugman, Paul, 166
Ku Klux Klan, 37
Kucinich, Dennis, 54, 163,
    168
Kurtz, David, 210

L
labor movement, 34
Laborde, Errol, 42
Landreth, Sonny, 43
Landrieu, Mary, 225
Landrieu, Mitch, 225
Landrieu, Moon, 225
Lane, Gary, 85
Lawrence, Chris, 51
Lawrence, Massachusetts, 34
Lee, Sheila Jackson, 62
Lee, Spike, 140, 144
Lent, 39
Lerner, Steve, 18
Leuchtenburg, William, 167
levees, 188–92, 212
Lewis, Peirce, 188
Long, Huey, 37, 45–46, 204
Lott, Trent, 3, 165
Louisiana Army Corps of
    Engineers, 166
Louisiana Purchase, 37
Lundquist, Andrew, 102
LVI Environmental Services,
    210

M
Mann, Phyllis, 112
Mann, Pleasant, 12
Mardi Gras, 39, 42–43
McCurry, Margaret, 172
McKibben, Bill, 19
Melkonian, Marilyn, 172
Mencken, H.L., 38–39
Mexico City earthquake, 150
Meyerson, Harold, 101
migrant labor, 207–10
Miller, Gary, 68
Miller, T. Christian, 96
Milton Eisenhower
    Foundation, 168
Milton, Walter, 224
Mississippi River, 18
mitigation grants, 13
Moffett, David, 112
Montgomery, Michael, 75–76
Morrow, Betty Hearn, 5–6
MSNBC, 51
Muhammad, Curtis, 149–50
Musgrave, Marilyn, 67
music, 40, 44, 139–46
Mystick Krewe of Comus, 42

N
NAACP, 137, 221
Nagin, Ray, 180–82, 192, 201,
    225
    evacuation, 61
    and Hispanics, 209

housing, 71–72
Naison, Mark, 167
National Organization of
    Minority Architects, 172
Negroponte, John, 74
Neocon kindergarten, 97
Neville, Aaron, 40
New Bridge Strategies, LLC, 102
New Deal, 45, 161–64, 167
New Orleans
    demographics of, 60–62
    geography of, 186–89
    history of, 35–44, 185–91
    housing, 71–72
    jail, 109–16
    and poverty, 50
    rebuilding, 61–62, 147–60,
        169–72, 186–87, 191
New York City, 6
Ninth Ward, 4, 7, 154

O

Obama, Barack, 78
O'Connor, Sandra Day, 43
oil supply, 89–93
OMB, 41
Operation Blessing, 81–85
Operation USA, 82
O'Reilly, Bill, 52

P

Paul, Ron, 69
Pelosi, Nancy, 28, 135

Pence, Mike, 64
People's Hurricane Fund, 151,
    217
Percy, Walker, 39
petrochemical factories, 18
PFM (Prison Fellowship Min-
    istries), 83–84
Pleasure Club, 42
Poe, Ted, 69
poverty, 5, 23–25, 34, 44–48,
    167
Prince, Edgar, 78
Prince, Erik, 78–79
Prince Group, 79
prisoners, 109–16
*Pro-Free-Market Ideas for
    Responding to Hurricane
    Katrina and High Gas
    Prices*, 64, 67–70
Progressive Era, 34
Project Impact, 13
The Purpose-Driven Life, 52

Q

Quinn, F. Patrick, 75

R

racism, 5, 9, 15, 29–31, 226
    See also African Americans
Rahim, Malik, 8, 15
Rathke, Wade, 135, 137
Ratner, Michael, 75
RealClimate.org, 20

rebuilding, 61–62, 147–60,
169–72, 186–87, 193
Reconstruction, 36
Reconstruction Finance
Corporation, 163
Red Cross, 82, 184
Reed, Adolph, Jr., 27
Reiss, James, 76, 181–82
Reiss, Jimmy, 148
relief efforts, 59–65, 147–51
Republicans, 78, 166, 175
Rex, 43
Rice, Condoleezza, 51
Riford, Rosie Lee, 158
Roberts, John G., 85
Robertson, Gordon, 86–87
Robertson, Pat, 81–87
Rogers, Ed, 102
Rohrabacher, Dana, 69
Romanov, Alexis Alexandrovich,
42
Roosevelt, Franklin, 45
Rove, Karl, 130
Ruffins, Kermit, 40
Rumsfeld, Donald, 181
Ruthie the Duck Girl, 38
Ryan, Paul, 67

S
The Sahara of the Bozart, 38
Sanchez, Mercedes, 207
Sanger, Margaret, 34
Santorum, Rick, 78
Saxon, Lyle, 41

Scheer, Robert, 45, 166
Schmitz, Joseph, 79
Scientology, 59, 64–65
security companies, 75
Seko, Mobutu Sese, 83
Selma, Alabama, 33
Sensenbrenner bill, 207
Shadegg, John, 69–70
Shaw Group, Inc., 98, 160
shelters, 133–37
Sizemore, Bill, 83
slavery, 197–98, 210
Smith, Shephard, 52
Southern Decadence
Weekend, 39
Southern Poverty Law
Center, 210
Sri Lanka, 150
St. Bernard Parish, 15
Steinbeck, John, 207
Stephens, Christine, 136
St. Tammany Parish, 37
Suber, Malcolm, 62–63
Superdome, 54
Swaggart, Jimmy, 38

T
Taylor, Charles, 84
Taylor, Danielle, 191
Tiahrt, Todd, 67, 69
Tigerman, Stanley, 172
Tine, Kirk Van, 104
TMO, 137
Tocqueville, Alexis de, 200

Travels With Charley, 207
Tubbs, Stephanie, 163
Twelfth Night Revelers, 42

U
Urban Homesteading Act, 63
Use Me, 59

V
Vanguard Public
    Foundation, 151
Vidrine, Jennifer, 126–28
Ville Platte, 119–21, 127, 129,
    184
Vitter, David, 205
voting rights, 37, 217–19
Voting Rights Act of 1965, 37,
    220

W
Wackenhut, 75
Walden, Richard, 82

Warren, Rick, 52
Welch, Jack, 171
wetlands, 18
White, Bill, 136
Wilkie, Curtis, 35
Williams, Joe, 145
Williams, Patricia J., 3
Williams, Tennessee, 39
Willis, Mark, 213
Withers, Bill, 59
Witt, James Lee, 12–13
Wolshon, Brian, 50
Worker Recovery Accounts, 204
WPA, 167

Y
Young, Andrew, 37

Z
Zahn, Paula, 51–52
Zulu King, 42
Zulu Social Aid, 42

ACKNOWLEDGMENTS

This book would not exist without its contributors, who responded generously and creatively to the human crisis and journalistic challenge presented by Hurricane Katrina. Some are longtime *Nation* writers; others were new to our pages. The vital presence of Southern voices reflects the editorial hand of Bob Moser, a North Carolina native who arrived in *The Nation*'s New York office to become acting senior editor in the fall of 2005. (The former editor of Durham's *Independent Weekly*, he is now editorial director of The Nation Institute's Investigative Fund and a contributing writer to the magazine.)

Many other pieces were edited with care and insight by Roane Carey, *The Nation*'s senior editor and copy chief. Joan Connell, *The Nation*'s Web editor, brought in the online-only content. Tom Engelhardt, founder of The Nation Institute's Tomdispatch.com, kindly permitted the reproduction of two pieces from his site. In countless ways the crucial work of *The Nation*'s staff, including interns Rachel Corbett and Garrett Ordower, and copy editor Mark Sorkin, is exhibited here. And the entire volume embodies the guiding editorial vision of *Nation* editor Katrina vanden Heuvel.

Special thanks also to Naomi Klein, Jeremy Scahill and Richard Kim for editorial advice; to The Nation Institute for essential support; and to Ruth Baldwin and Carl Bromley at Nation Books for bringing to bear their inimitable combination of style, humor, enthusiasm, erudition, and administrative wizardry to make it all happen on deadline (more or less).